AF344446

SEE THE OZARKS

WHERE TO GO IN THE OZARKS
by KEITH McCANSE
THIRD ANNUAL EDITION
SPECIAL EDITION
AUTOMOBILE CLUB OF MISSOURI
GENERAL OFFICES
4228 LINDELL BLVD.
ST. LOUIS, MO.
AUTO CLUB MISSOURI
AAA
50¢
"A THOUSAND AND ONE PLACES TO GO"
1930 PUBLICATION
"THE LAND OF A MILLION SMILES"
SOUTHWEST MISSOURI
PLAYGROUNDS OF THE OZARKS
NORTHEAST OKLAHOMA
NORTHWEST ARKANSAS
Ozark Playgrounds Assn. Tourist Bureau, Joplin, Mo.
MISSOURI'S
Lake of the OZARKS
The OZARKS
The Land of a Million Smiles
GREETINGS
LAKE NORFORK
IN THE BEAUTIFUL OZARKS

Leland & Crystal Payton

SEE THE OZARKS

THE TOURISTIC IMAGE

Lens & Pen Press

Dedicated to John Margolies, whose many wonderful books on the American roadside and popular culture have been an inspiration. Thanks for your sage advice through the years.

First Edition. Printed in Singapore

All illustrations are from the collection of Leland & Crystal Payton, unless noted

ISBN: 0-9673925-1-9
Library of Congress Control Number: 2002094474

Lens & Pen Press
P.O. Box 14557
Springfield, MO 65814

Visit our web site: www.beautifulozarks.com

Typesetting and prepress by Ross Payton
ross@slangdesign.com

Leland & Crystal Payton have written 10 books on the Ozarks and popular culture. They have two sons, Ross, an electronic and video artist, and Strader, a teacher in Japan.

CONTENTS

The Ozark Hills Are Calling Me
by May Stafford Hilburn
KIMBALL - HILBURN, PUBLISHERS
JEFFERSON CITY, MISSOURI.
PRICE-30¢ NET
OZARK MTS.
Vacationeland

MARVEL CAVE
SHEPHERD OF THE HILLS COUNTRY
ENTRANCE TO GREAT CATHEDRAL

Sammy Lane
BOAT LINE & RESORT
H.G. McQuerfer
Manager
Branson, Missouri

A SPORTING PARADISE

A Typical Float Scene in the Scenic Ozarks

Sportsmen were the first to travel to the Ozarks to recreate. Isolated from the progress that was changing much of America, the hilly regions of Missouri and Arkansas gained, in the late 1800s, a reputation as a hunting and fishing paradise that endures to this day. Eastern journals extolled the quality of an Ozarkian outdoor adventure.

The Ozark streams afford a wide field for the canoeist, and besides being easily accessible to those who live in the Middle West, this section of Missouri is almost unequaled in beauty of scenery and wealth of fishing and hunting.

– *Recreation* magazine, September 1909

Ozark Ripley, in his 1922 magazine article, "The Alluring Ozarks," lauds an indigenous hill country pursuit: floating and

Scale model johnboat (above). At the height of his float fishing business, Branson entrepreneur Jim Owen had 40 such boats operating on six rivers and streams.

Most early sporting forays in the Ozarks were all-male affairs. Real photo postcard (right) circa 1920.

THE FISHERMEN'S DRAY & TWO JOLLY SPORTSMEN
BACK FROM THE JAMES RIVER, GALENA MO.   732 HALL PHOTO CO.

fishing from a johnboat. Long, narrow, and originally made from native pine, these craft evolved, some speculate, from the southern pirogue. Flat-bottomed, with a shallow draft, the johnboat was ideal for negotiating the swift, shallow riffles that connected deep, green pools full of goggle-eye and "brownies" (smallmouth bass). Ripley credits another important component of the classic float trip: the native guide. Hillfolk not only knew the country, they were renowned for their tall tales and country wit. Many, like Charlie Barnes, an early float guide, also built the johnboats.

> There is but one ideal method of fishing the Ozarks . . . the float trip. No better craft for all Ozark fishing purposes has been designed than a typical Ozark johnboat. Ozark guides are amenable fellows for their four dollars a day. The railroads traversing the Ozarks are prompt to provide campers with guides that are dependable.

When the White River Railway reached the hamlets of Hollister and Branson, a group of well-to-do St. Louis sportsmen erected a most impressive clubhouse on a bluff overlooking the river. The Maine Club, as they called themselves, bought, dismantled, and shipped by rail the State of Maine's exhibit building for the 1904 St. Louis World's Fair. Occupied by the club less than ten years, the property was sold to the School (now College) of the Ozarks. Legend has it, the members' wives cared little for outdoorsy recreation, and found Branson and Hollister provincial. The well-traveled, spacious log lodge burned in 1930.

Roughing it appealed to few women. But when amenities like private rooms, screen doors, wood floors, and sometimes even plumbing, began appearing in rustic resorts, wives began to accompany husbands on Ozarks sporting trips. By the 1920s, road-building allowed automobiles access to some scenic wild spots such as Roaring River, near Cassville. Many tourists still took the train, but were then delivered to the resort by car or bus.

Eureka Springs hosted a dandy Gun Club (above). The native hunter and his dogs (left) were intriguing to early tourists, as this circa 1910 postcard shows. Both country and urban outdoorsmen have long found the Ozarks a sporting paradise.

Dobyns Hall, originally the Maine Club, was built by a group of St. Louis sportsmen. Adirondacks-style structures like this were in vogue with American outdoorsmen in the Teddy Roosevelt era. This rustic architecture never died out in the Ozarks. The Bass Pro organization conspicuously carries on the tradition today.

Roaring River's ambitious complex offered both trout fishing and dancing. Kansas City entrepreneur R. E. Bruner developed the resort, but lost it to foreclosure in 1928. St. Louis soap magnate, Dr. Thomas M. Sayman bought it at auction for $105,000. He sold it to the state for $1. It is now a state park.

Stock the Ozarks with Wild Turkeys

The hills and forests of the Ozarks are ideal for wild turkeys. If they have been shot out in your favorite section restock with genuine wild turkey stock from Lost Trail Lodge.

Your interest may be in a private preserve, or as a member of a hunting and fishing club that desires to improve its hunting. Individuals will appreciate these turkeys.

A Product of Lost Trail Lodge

For Information and Prices, Address

B. K. LEACH
1821 Railway Exchange Bldg.
ST. LOUIS, MO.

Lost Trail Lodge in the Ozarks

The Ozarks has been covered by national sporting publications since the 1800s. It remains a famed sportsman's paradise.

Rail development not only gave sportsmen access to the Ozarks, it made commercial exploitation of game possible. By the early 1900s, habitat loss and market hunting began depleting game populations, which alarmed sportsmen. Regulations would clearly be required. The Missouri Game and Fish Department (later renamed the Missouri Department of Conservation) was one of the nation's earliest scientifically managed and apolitically run government agencies to administer a state's natural resources. Ozarks private game preserves had developed restocking techniques that were implemented statewide. The August 1927 *Missouri Game and Fish News* reports a foresighted mission: the acquisition of some of the Ozarks great springs for parks. Clearly, sportsmen cared about the region's beauty.

Canyons, deep falling and walled by precipitous cliffs. Pine clad summits and ranges towering for miles above winding gorges in which rivers flow, now with deliberate majesty over beckoning depths, now rushing with terrifying haste down narrow rock strewn banks and beds on their way to the Great Outside. Clear mountain streams laughing over gravelled bottoms, and spray-hung falls sun-transformed into miniature rainbows as their crystal waters dash to the pool below where rainbow trout tempt the angler's skill. Broken landscapes of rugged hills, complaining brooks and pensive vales and quiet woods in whose fastnesses are the wild turkey and the deer.

Ozark Life Outdoors (right page) was focused specifically on the region. Publication began in the travel boom of the mid 1920s; the magazine folded during the Depression. Along with some let's-go-fishing-for-smallmouth-on-the-Niangua-River-type articles, there were impassioned editorials calling for the reform of any remaining unenlightened and highly politicized fish and game department policies.

The political ads for the race for governor of Missouri in 1932 have a familiar ring. Democrat Russell L. Dearmont was "an expert fisherman and fly caster," while Republican Charles U. Becker assured sportsmen of his "interest for game and fish development." Conservation issues got public attention. Clearly, the affluent, literate, well-traveled urban sportsman was a voter who counted. That citizen cared deeply about the primitive Ozarks as a recreational resource.

THE SPOTS WERE SCENIC AND THE SPORT WAS GOOD ON OUR TRIP

(Photos by Guy W. Von Schriltz)

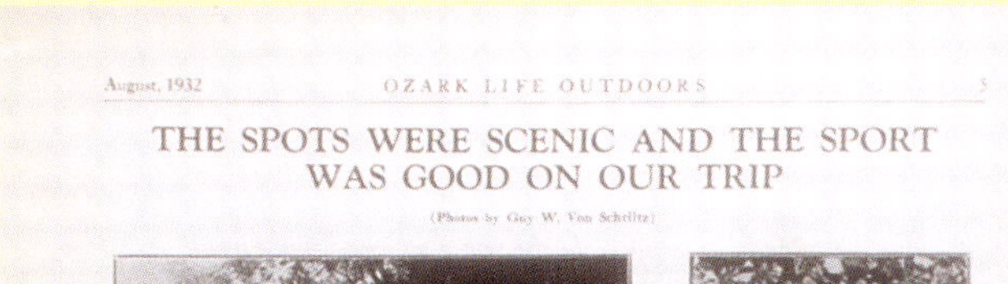

NATE'S CABIN

18½-INCH MISSOURI RAINBOW TROUT FROM NIANGUA RIVER

NATE

THIS FISH WAS WIDE AND HEAVY, SOLID TOBACCO BROWN, AN INCH LONGER THAN "OUR HOMEMADE LANDING NET"

INDIAN GRAVE BLUFF ON THE NIANGUA
INDIAN GRAVE EDDY BELOW IT

(Continued from Page 9)

Chief of Hatchery, salary and expenses, office and miscellaneous supplies, etc. ... 6,069.23

Fish food, insurance, repairs, oil, gas, supplies, etc. ... 11,585.70

Total ... $43,286.39

Thus we find in the Hatchery Division that salaries and travel expenses are $31,700.69, and fish food and miscellaneous, $11,585.70.

We make a recapitulation of some of the above figures and find that expenditures are:

Protection Division, salaries ... $ 83,393.81

Protection Division, travel expenses ... 63,371.07

Hatchery Division, salaries and traveling expenses ... 31,700.69

$178,465.57

A total of nearly one-half of the revenue being spent for salaries and traveling expenses from the fund maintained by sportsmen in the state.

The total cost of the Hatchery Division operation for 1931 was $43,286.39, and 1,921,456 fish were produced and distributed. With these figures, we find that it cost $44.40 per thousand fish released in streams and lakes of Missouri.

All figures with one exception are taken from the Annual Report of 1931 by Commissioner John H. Ross. The exception being that where 92 people drew approximately $97,864 per year for salaries, this being taken from the Missouri Manual (Blue Book).

The above article is not intended as a tirade against the personnel of the State Game and Fish Department but is intended to bring home the fact that the present method of using the department as a political housecleaning hull should be stopped and make of the department one that will be on par with some of the thirty-one other states that have such forms of management. It is our belief that a bipartisan Commission will help solve some of the problems of successfully carrying through to completion a more thorough operating program of game propagation and fish culture.

Sportsman and Advocate of Proper Conservation of Wild Life Resources

VOTE FOR

CHAS. U. BECKER

Republican Candidate For Governor

Sportsmen Assured of Becker's Interest for Game and Fish Development

Mr. Becker has promised to continue his efforts in behalf of Missouri's best interests in the matter of fish and game and her public parks and playgrounds. In his platform of principles he states that he will see that our streams and lakes are kept restocked and will put game back into our forests, to meet the increasing requirements of our own sportsmen and the thousands of tourists from other states. He advocates many small native fish hatchery ponds at the sources of all large game fish streams. He points out the fact that this can be done cheaply in the wild lands around our innumerable large springs and headwaters of our streams.

THIS SPACE SPONSORED BY SPORTSMEN FRIENDS OF BECKER FOR GOVERNOR

ANIMAL DRAWINGS

ILLUSTRATIONS — LETTERING AND DESIGNS
For All Occasions
SATISFIED CUSTOMERS IN MANY STATES

GUY OEHLER

Kansas City,   2538 Denver Avenue   Missouri
YOU'LL FIND MY PRICES MOST REASONABLE

SUBSCRIBE FOR THE
American Pigeon Journal
FRANK H. HOLLMANN, Editor
12 MONTHS' Subscription **$1.00**

AMERICAN PIGEON JOURNAL CO.
DEPT. O.   WARRENTON, MO.

SEE PAGES 16 AND 17
ON FREE
OZARK VACATIONS

SPORTSMEN VOTE FOR

RUSSELL L. DEARMONT

Democratic Candidate for Governor

He stands for a Commission Form of State Game and Fish Department, as shown by his record

He is an ardent sportsman and believes in proper methods of game and fish conservation

SENATOR DEARMONT'S RECORD SHOWS

That during the last session of the State Legislature when a bill advocating a commission form of State Game and Fish Department was introduced, he made a speech in defense of it.

AN EXPERT FISHERMAN AND FLY CASTER

Senator Dearmont is a great lover of the outdoors and whenever the opportunity offers he may be seen fishing along some of the streams of the state. He is a champion of the sportsman's cause and deserves the sportsman's vote.

A VOTE FOR DEARMONT MEANS ADDED STRENGTH TO THE SPORTSMEN'S FIGHT FOR A COMMISSION FORM OF GAME AND FISH DEPARTMENT FOR MISSOURI

This Space Sponsored by

SPORTSMEN FRIENDS OF DEARMONT FOR GOVERNOR

Missouri Game & Fish Department

Keith McCanse

State Game and Fish Commissioner

Jefferson City, Missouri.

Game Refuges

Play in Missouri

Dear Friend of the Outdoors:-

Your request for a State Park folder is enough to tell us that you are a lover of God's great outdoors and all that it holds.

Missouri offers everything the lover of nature could possibly wish. You need seek no further. What nature has put here belongs to us all to enjoy - to use, but not to abuse.

There are fish in our streams, birds and wild creatures in our forests. Myriad stately trees, wild flowers and bubbling brooks delight the visitor at every turn. The rugged bluffs, inspiring landscapes and crystal clear rivers characterize the Ozark region.

Fishing and hunting; rest and recreation are here. Enjoy yourself. Play in Missouri.

Write me if there is any information you want not covered in the enclosed literature. We want to help you enjoy Missouri.

Yours for Conservation,

Keith McCanse

State Game and Fish Commissioner.

State Parks are a Part of This Department, Being Financed Through Sale of Hunting and Fishing Licenses

State Parks

Fish Hatcheries

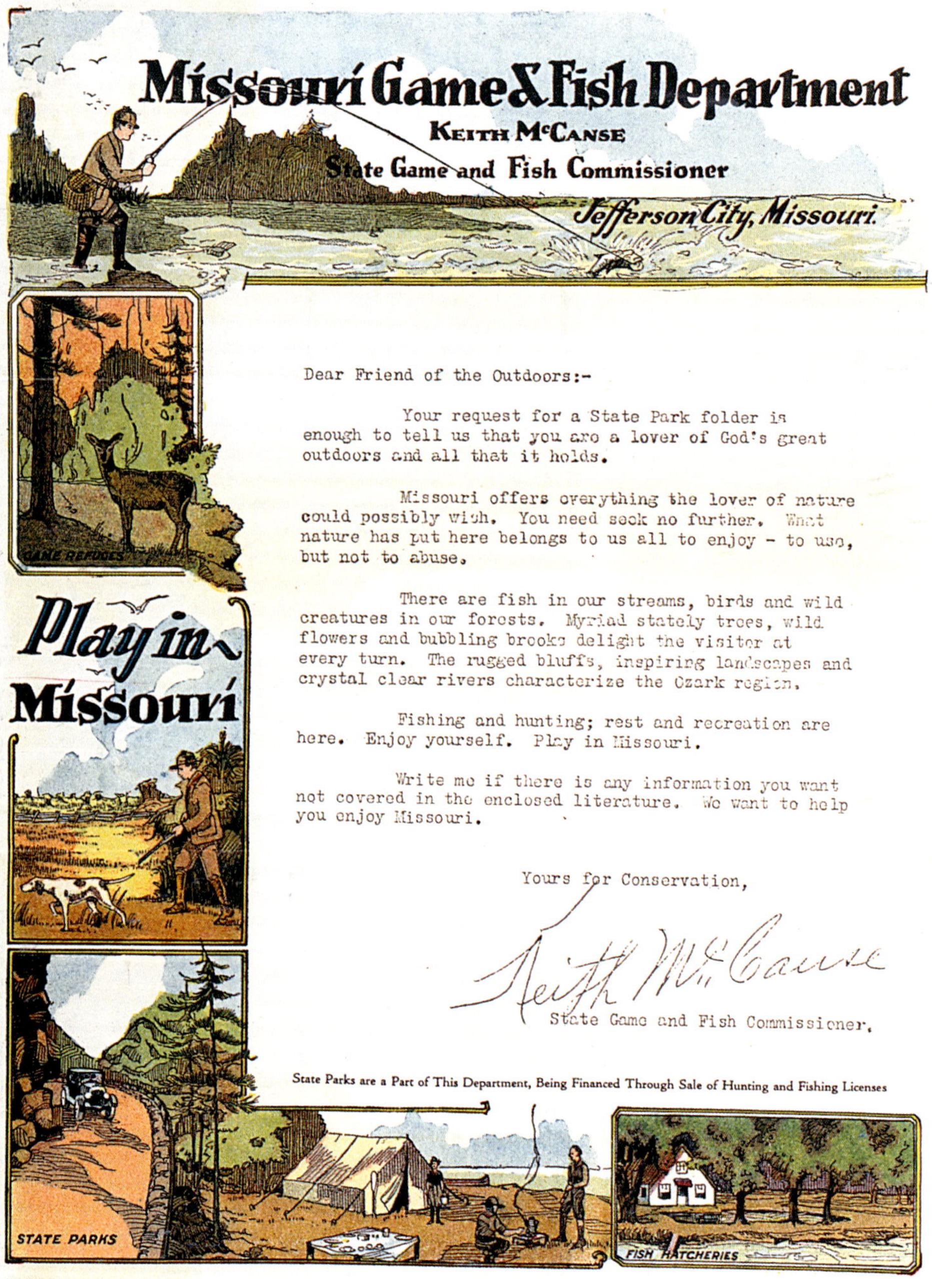

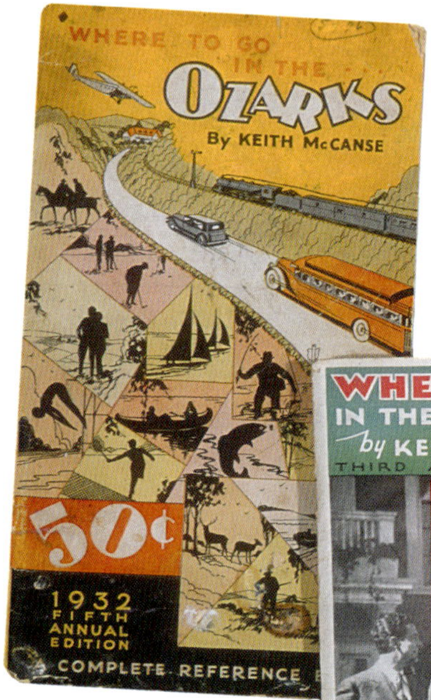

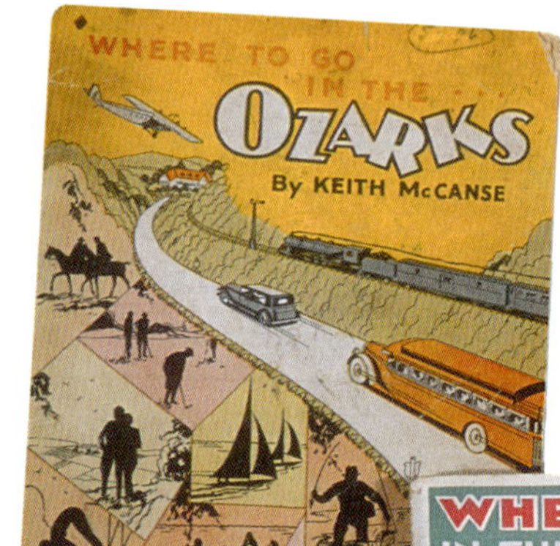

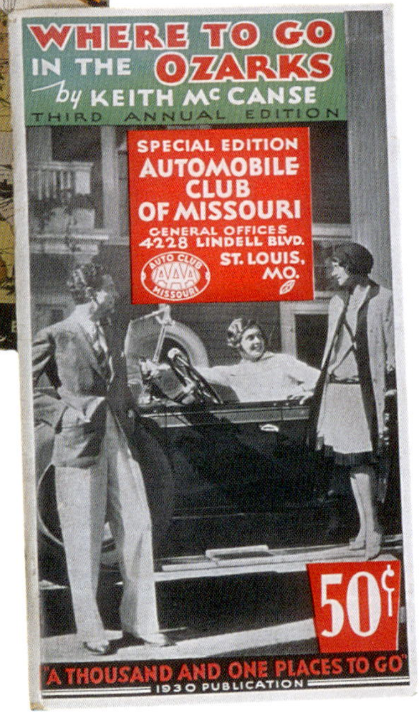

Dancing or fishing? A few years ago, it was all hunting, fishing, and camping. Ozarks meant outdoor life in the rough with no alternative. Today, it's different. The dancers, representing those vacationists who like a round of golf, the comforts of a modern resort, some horseback riding, tennis, archery and touring, will find the Ozarks offering every type of attraction and accommodation.

In the prosperous 1920s, Ozarks tourism diversified. Keith McCanse pointed this out in his comprehensive 1930s *Where To Go In The Ozarks.* Better roads, the phenomenal growth in automobile ownership, and new businesses that catered to tourists were graphically illustrated in this 130-page travel guide.

McCanse, a descendant of Ozark pioneers, was the former reform-minded commissioner of the Missouri Game and Fish Department. He acknowledged the new recreational interests, but didn't forget that sportsmen discovered the place and continued to be major players in the new touristic mix.

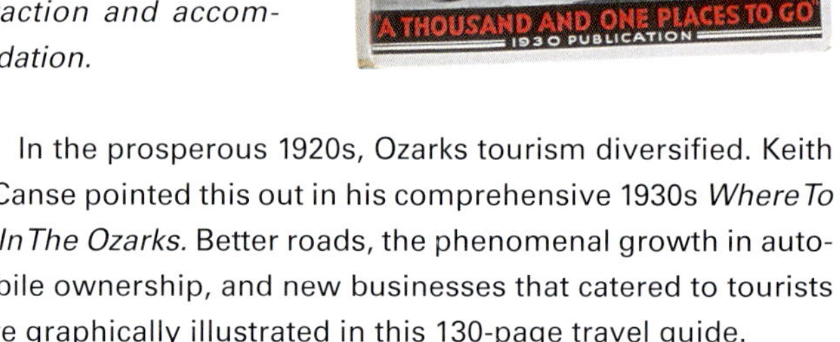

Daniel Boone and the early trail-blazing pioneers found the Ozarks so attractive that this region at one time was the most populous area west of the Mississippi River.

Since that early day the Ozarks have developed. They now have their towns, cities, and thriving communities, agricultural and industrial developments but, in the background, out in the hills there remains the forests, the streams, caves, and springs that appealed so strongly to the frontier-men.

McCanse clearly understood the deep cultural roots of hunting and fishing in America and often referred to the Ozarks in his guidebooks as a "Sportman's Paradise."

Images of outdoor sports remain prominent in the advertising of Ozark tourism for good reason. Hunters and fishermen paid for the first parks and preserves. Outdoorsmen like McCanse transformed a good-old-boy bureaucracy into a scientifically managed conservation department. Game restocking, along with regulation, reversed many kinds of decline in wildlife. Those who fish, hunt, camp, and canoe have done much to insure that the wild Ozarks will always be a sporting paradise.

After modernizing the structure of the Game and Fish Department, Keith McCanse ran a small touristic conglomerate. He was an outdoors radio commentator, an Ozark guidebook publisher, and an early investor in Lake of the Ozarks recreation. The Depression adversely affected this venture and McCanse left Missouri. He resettled in Texas where he became successful in real estate and prominent in Republican politics.

Many float trips began at Galena before Table Rock Lake backed up the lower James River in 1960. They ended 125 river miles downstream at Branson. Smallmouth bass were the primary quarry, but, as this real photo postcard shows, big catfish were not unknown.

For 50 years, Ozark Ripley (James B. Thompson) was a famous outdoor writer. He hunted and fished the world over, but his fondest memories were of his childhood johnboat floats with his father on the Eleven Point and Current rivers.

EUREKA SPRINGS

No rusticated place this. Improbably built into the side of some of the Arkansas Ozarks' steepest real estate is an authentic Victorian village. One hundred years ago, nattily attired ladies and gentlemen strolled miles of winding paths along hand-cut stone walls, pausing to sip the waters of the various springs. Each was held to have particular medicinal powers. Eureka Springs called itself "The City That Water Built."

Twenty-first century tourists are considerably more casually dressed. Few believe the spring waters will cure anything but the thirst that comes from touring "the stair step town" on foot.

"The city of healing waters—there's health in every glass," proclaims the World War I era pamphlet (left), its pages shaped like a tumbler. The booklet's testimonials about diseases cured by Eureka's springs fall flat now, but the boasts of the place's overall attractiveness hold up.

The lure of the Ozarks and the all-year charm of Eureka Springs as a place of restful enjoyment is not alone for those who journey in quest of health. The country surrounding Eureka Springs is a great shaded park and playground, a land of hills and valleys arched with translucent blue on its many cloudless days.

Born Spring

Well-to-do and aspiring middle-class types flocked to the place from the Midwest and the South to socialize and recreate. A handsome 80-year-old gilt stamped brochure exalts the picturesque Ozark countryside that hotel guests explored.

The whole country about Eureka Springs abounds in the beauties of Nature. Towering mountains of green; huge rugged cliffs; gushing springs, murmuring brooks, rocks of all sorts of strange and curious constructions; caves of most singular and interesting formation; gulches and vales, filled with almost every conceivable variety of scenery, charm and inspire the traveler who takes a ride or drive in any direction. A different trip may be taken every day in the month without exhausting this wonder field of nature.

Horseback riding to view the Ozarkian vistas was wildly popular. Large parties would ride far out into the country, have a prepared picnic lunch, and return to an evening of concerts, dancing, and, in some cases, making the acquaintance of a member of the opposite sex of suitable social standing.

Old Eureka was an odd mixture of vigorous traditional, outdoorsy pursuits and luxurious comforts aided by up-to-date technology. The Crescent Livery Stables, which supplied riding horses and carriages, had a telephone system hooked up in 1895 to the better hotels. This enabled owner J.W. Hill to fulfill the exact needs of his fickle, well-to-do clientele. Gas lighting was available by 1885. As early as 1891, coal-fired steam generation systems supplied electricity to the little resort town. A few years later, the mule-drawn streetcars were electrified. Presumably, the let-go mules went back to pulling the plow in tiny vegetable gardens in the rugged hills that surround the town.

Photographs (above) from a turn-of-the-century album (above and center) titled *Glimpses of Eureka*. Guests enjoyed both bracing tours of nature and the refined accommodations of the many hotels.

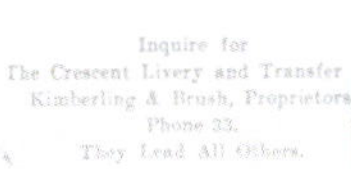

A hand-painted plate, made in Germany, and sterling silver souvenir spoon (right) memorialized an odd chunk of limestone known as Pivot Rock.

Out for a Morning Ride.

Over 100 hotels have operated in Eureka Springs' 120-year history. Many, like the Southern Hotel, exist today only as images on plates like the one above, hand painted in Germany, or on old postcards. Amenities originally offered by the 100-room Crescent Hotel (still in business) included steam heat, baths, electric lights, elevator, sun parlor, orchestra, tennis, billiards, bowling alleys and a sun room. Rates in 1918 were $2 to $4 a day.

The real story of Eureka Springs is as winding and up and down as its streets. A slapdash boomtown popped up in the late 1870s when claims were made about the miraculous medicinal properties of the springs that seeped from the steep hills. Powell Clayton, a former Union officer in the Civil War, with the help of other Republican friends, transformed a motley assemblage of tents and shacks into an upscale spa with its own railroad.

General Clayton, as he was called, had ridden Reconstruction politics into the office of Governor of Arkansas, then U.S. Senator, but eventually he felt the heat of the re-enfranchised electorate. After his brother was assassinated and several attempts were made on his own life, Clayton hightailed it out of Little Rock with a carpetbag full of money. He then devoted his considerable energies to creating the fantasy resort that is Eureka Springs.

Clayton's showplace was the neo-Gothic Crescent Hotel. Built of native limestone by imported Irish stonemasons on the top of a hill in 1886, it has survived use as a college and misuse as

The Basin Park Hotel, adjoining famous Basin Spring. One hundred choice rooms. W. M. Duncan, Proprietor.

a quack hospital. Happily, this "castle in the sky" has been restored to its earlier grandeur and is open again.

Next to one of Eureka's best known springs is the 1905 Basin Park Hotel. Each of its eight stories is "ground level," as it rises beside a cliff. Restored as well, this landmark still functions as a fine hotel. Basin Park Spring has been a favorite spot for musicians and visitors for over a century.

Eureka Springs today hosts jazz and blues festivals. Good country music shows have permanent theaters here as well. Its folk life festival is one of the Ozarks' oldest. Antique and gift shops line the winding streets. Since the 1930s, it's been known as a writers' and artists' colony. A short line, old-time tour train still operates, but it no longer delivers visitors in Edwardian clothes toting alligator suitcases.

Springs are common throughout the Ozarks. Some efforts to promote the medicinal benefits of drinking or bathing in their waters were made elsewhere in the region, but with much less success than at Eureka Springs. Few of these late 19th century enterprises had the scenery. None benefited from the ambition, imagination, and money of Powell Clayton and his associates. Even when there was widespread faith in the healing properties of the various waters, the ancillary pleasures of gracious accommodations, fine food, shopping and sightseeing gave Eureka Springs an edge over other purveyors of the water cure.

This 1909 postcard shaped like Missouri promoted "the health giving qualities of her natural springs."

Souvenir aluminum pin tray, circa 1900. Sulphur Springs was an early rival of Eureka Springs.

Bokert Water (left), a "natural mineral spring water" for "table and medicinal use," was bottled from a spring at DeSoto, Missouri south of St. Louis.

Since the late 1800s, Ozark spring waters have been commercially utilized. This 1920s tin sign (right) borrowed a slogan from the Ozark Playgrounds Association.

Monte Ne was an ambitious Ozarks resort that was not to be. All that is left are a few foundations on the bottom of Beaver Lake and near its shore, near Rogers, Arkansas.

William Hope Harvey made a fortune in Colorado real estate in the 1880s. In Chicago, he allied with William Jennings Bryan on the issue of free silver. Known as "Coin" Harvey, he published a wildly successful series of little pulp books on money. Around 1900, he relocated to the Ozarks and constructed his fantasy recreational complex about twenty miles west of flourishing Eureka Springs.

Wealthy recreationalists could arrive by a train that ran on a spur he had constructed. Costumed gondoliers then poled the well-heeled to rustic 350 foot long "cabins." Monte Ne had its own bank, golf course, enclosed swimming pool and fabulous ballroom.

In an effort to attract the growing numbers of automobile- driv-

reveal "the cause of the death of a former civilization."

Too few guests appreciated Monte Ne's unusual charms. Financial problems beset the aging visionary. He died in 1936, before either the structure or the book it was to protect were completed.

ing travelers, Col. Harvey organized the Ozark Trails Association in 1913 to mark and promote 1,500 miles of automobile highways in the region. All of the roads were routed out of Monte Ne. However, unlike train-delivered guests, the freedom of movement provided by private transportation meant that automobile tourists didn't stay long in one resort, including Monte Ne.

In 1925, Harvey began to build a huge pyramid which, he said, "would house the secrets of our civilization." These secrets would be contained in a 400-page book which he claimed would

OPPORTUNITY IN THE OZARKS

Sportsmen and vacationers were not the only groups invited to come and see the Ozarks. The Frisco Line's full-page, color ad (page 25) in a 1912 Washington, DC, *Star Sunday Magazine* asked, "why don't you take your family to live in the beautiful Ozarks?"

A small farm in the Ozarks is the opportunity you need. Think what a wholesome, healthy life it would mean for your children. You can get a small place near good towns, and good schools, as low as $10 per acre.

Through the decades, Ozarks promotional material often mixed appeals to both vacationers and would-be immigrants. Visitors today are seen as potential buyers of condos or second homes. After a lifetime as summer visitors, many people come to live in the region when they retire. Others, who spent their childhood in the Ozarks and their working lives in far-away cities, often return to their roots.

The earliest railroad promotions appealed to small farmers, even "the hundreds of city men now struggling against the 'high cost of living' who would find the Ozarks one practical avenue

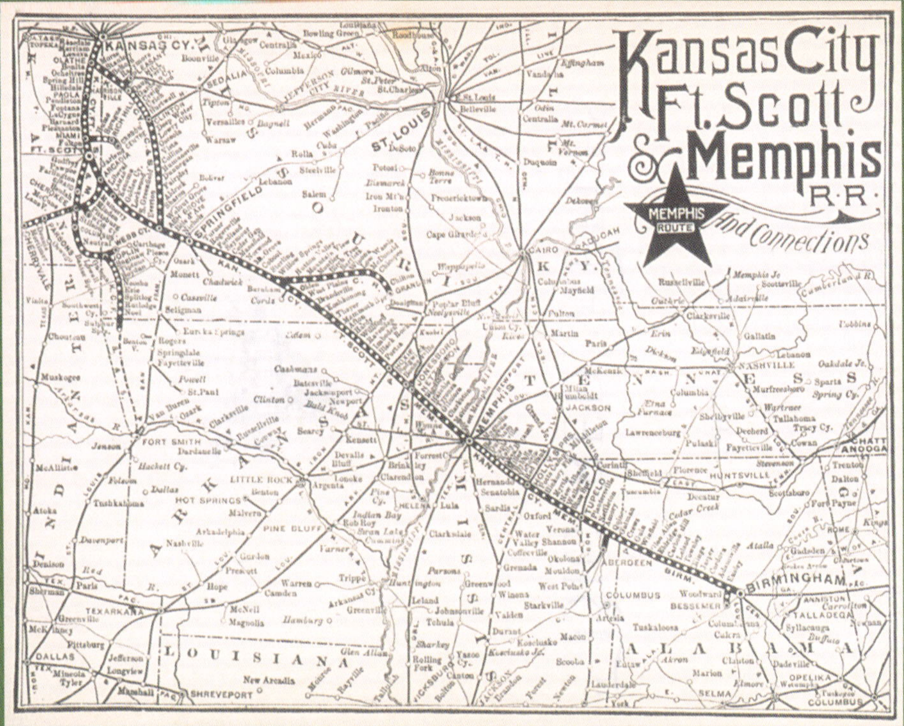

Railroads provided access to city markets for labor-intensive produce like apples, strawberries, and tomatoes. These crops were suited to Ozark soils.

OZARK
OPPORTUNITIES
IN
"The Land of a Million Smiles"
One of the Smiles
W. A. King Realty Sales Co.
SUCCESSORS TO
BOSTON MOUNTAIN DEVELOPMENT CO.
FAYETTEVILLE
ARKANSAS

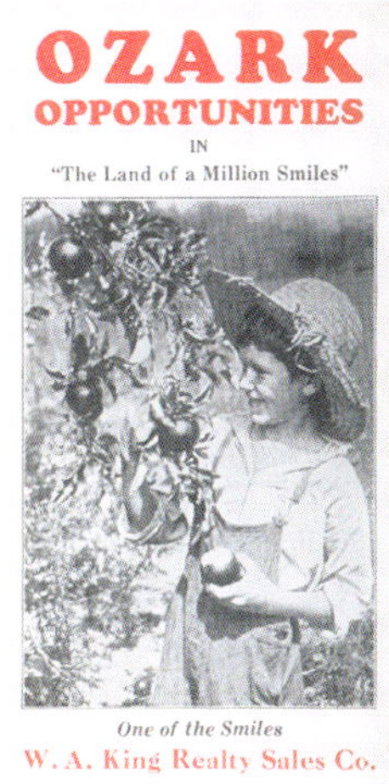

for going 'back to the farm.'" The legacy of such advertisements remains a part of the touristic image of the Ozarks. It is perceived to be a place friendly to the aspirations of the average family man, "willing to work hard and desiring an independent life."

Laura Ingalls Wilder, author of the *Little House* books, and her husband Almanzo were typical of these late nineteenth- and early twentieth-century settlers. She and Manny bought their farm, Rocky Ridge, near Mansfield in 1894. They practiced progressive farming and she wrote her classic books on pioneer family life.

Much of the hilly Ozarks is unsuitable for row crop agriculture. For a time, it was a major producer of fruits and specialty crops, like strawberries and tomatoes. As early as the 1870s, the rail corporations enthusiastically promoted the Ozarks as "The Land of Big Red Apples." Some orchards have survived, but the region's importance as a source of these labor-intensive products has declined. The dominant farm activities today are raising cattle and, in some sectors, poultry.

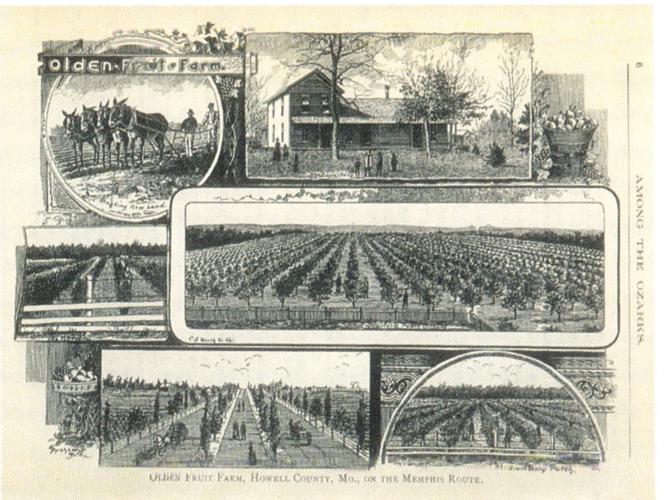

Olden·Fruit·Farm.
AMONG THE OZARKS
6
OLDEN FRUIT FARM, HOWELL COUNTY, MO., ON THE MEMPHIS ROUTE.

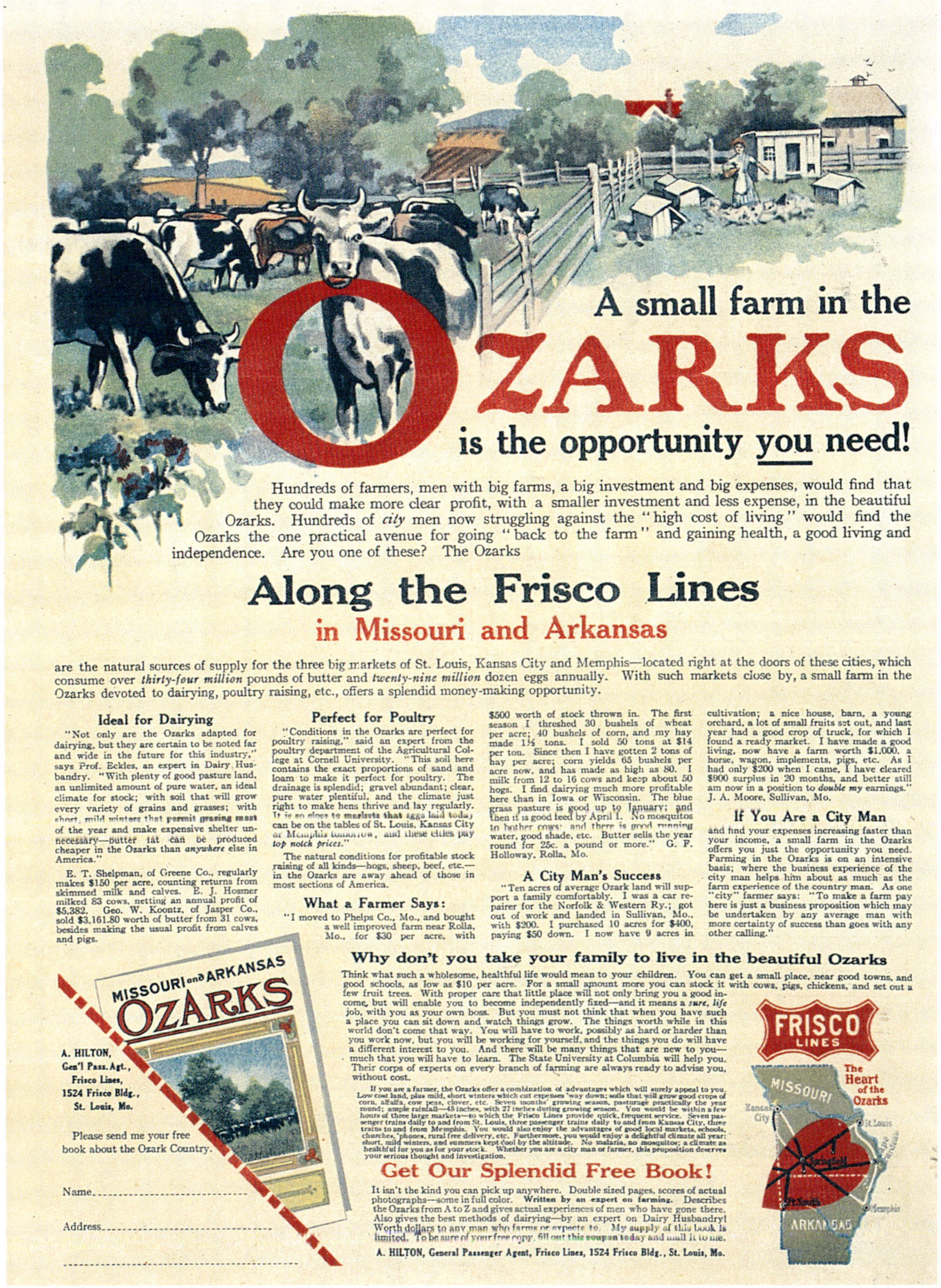

A small farm in the
OZARKS
is the opportunity you need!
Hundreds of farmers, men with big farms, a big investment and big expenses, would find that they could make more clear profit, with a smaller investment and less expense, in the beautiful Ozarks. Hundreds of city men now struggling against the "high cost of living" would find the Ozarks the one practical avenue for going "back to the farm" and gaining health, a good living and independence. Are you one of these? The Ozarks
Along the Frisco Lines
in Missouri and Arkansas
are the natural sources of supply for the three big markets of St. Louis, Kansas City and Memphis—located right at the doors of these cities, which consume over thirty-four million pounds of butter and twenty-nine million dozen eggs annually. With such markets close by, a small farm in the Ozarks devoted to dairying, poultry raising, etc., offers a splendid money-making opportunity.
Ideal for Dairying
"Not only are the Ozarks adapted for dairying, but they are certain to be noted far and wide in the future for this industry," says Prof. Eckles, an expert in Dairy Husbandry. "With plenty of good pasture land, an unlimited amount of pure water, an ideal climate for stock; with soil that will grow every variety of grains and grasses; with short, mild winters that permit grazing most of the year and make expensive shelter unnecessary—butter fat can be produced cheaper in the Ozarks than anywhere else in America."
E. T. Shelpman, of Greene Co., regularly makes $150 per acre, counting returns from skimmed milk and calves. E. J. Hosmer milked 83 cows, netting an annual profit of $5,382. Geo. W. Koontz, of Jasper Co., sold $3,161.80 worth of butter from 31 cows, besides making the usual profit from calves and pigs.
Perfect for Poultry
"Conditions in the Ozarks are perfect for poultry raising," said an expert from the poultry department of the Agricultural College at Cornell University. "This soil here contains the exact proportions of sand and loam to make it perfect for poultry. The drainage is splendid; gravel abundant; clear, pure water plentiful, and the climate just right to make hens thrive and lay regularly. It is so close to markets that eggs laid today can be on the tables of St. Louis, Kansas City or Memphis tomorrow, and these cities pay top notch prices."
The natural conditions for profitable stock raising of all kinds—hogs, sheep, beef, etc.—in the Ozarks are away ahead of those in most sections of America.
What a Farmer Says:
"I moved to Phelps Co., Mo., and bought a well improved farm near Rolla, Mo., for $30 per acre, with $500 worth of stock thrown in. The first season I threshed 30 bushels of wheat per acre; 40 bushels of corn, and my hay made 1½ tons. I sold 50 tons at $14 per ton. Since then I have gotten 2 tons of hay per acre; corn yields 65 bushels per acre now, and has made as high as 80. I milk from 12 to 16 cows and keep about 50 hogs. I find dairying much more profitable here than in Iowa or Wisconsin. The blue grass pasture is good up to January; and then it is good feed by April 1. No mosquitos to bother cows; and there is good running water, good shade, etc. Butter sells the year round for 25c. a pound or more." G. F. Holloway, Rolla, Mo.
A City Man's Success
"Ten acres of average Ozark land will support a family comfortably. I was a car repairer for the Norfolk & Western Ry.; got out of work and landed in Sullivan, Mo., with $200. I purchased 10 acres for $400, paying $50 down. I now have 9 acres in cultivation; a nice house, barn, a young orchard, a lot of small fruits set out, and last year had a good crop of truck, for which I found a ready market. I have made a good living, now have a farm worth $1,000, a horse, wagon, implements, pigs, etc. As I had only $200 when I came, I have cleared $900 surplus in 20 months, and better still am now in a position to double my earnings." J. A. Moore, Sullivan, Mo.
If You Are a City Man
and find your expenses increasing faster than your income, a small farm in the Ozarks offers you just the opportunity you need. Farming in the Ozarks is on an intensive basis; where the business experience of the city man helps him about as much as the farm experience of the country man. As one "city" farmer says: "To make a farm pay here is just a business proposition which may be undertaken by any average man with more certainty of success than goes with any other calling."
Why don't you take your family to live in the beautiful Ozarks
Think what such a wholesome, healthful life would mean to your children. You can get a small place, near good towns, and good schools, as low as $10 per acre. For a small amount more you can stock it with cows, pigs, chickens, and set out a few fruit trees. With proper care that little place will not only bring you a good income, but will enable you to become independently fixed—and it means a sure, life job, with you as your own boss. But you must not think that when you have such a place you can sit down and watch things grow. The things worth while in this world don't come that way. You will have to work, possibly as hard or harder than you work now, but you will be working for yourself, and the things you do will have a different interest to you. And there will be many things that are new to you—much that you will have to learn. The State University at Columbia will help you. Their corps of experts on every branch of farming are always ready to advise you, without cost.
If you are a farmer, the Ozarks offer a combination of advantages which will surely appeal to you. Low cost land, plus mild, short winters which cut expenses 'way down; soils that will grow good crops of corn, alfalfa, cow peas, clover, etc. Seven months' growing season, pasturage practically the year round; ample rainfall—45 inches, with 27 inches during growing season. You would be within a few hours of three large markets—to which the Frisco Lines provide quick, frequent service. Seven passenger trains daily to and from St. Louis, three passenger trains daily to and from Kansas City, three trains to and from Memphis. You would also enjoy the advantages of good local markets, schools, churches, 'phones, rural free delivery, etc. Furthermore, you would enjoy a delightful climate all year: short, mild winters, and summers kept cool by the altitude. No malaria, no mosquitos; a climate as healthful for you as for your stock. Whether you are a city man or farmer, this proposition deserves your serious thought and investigation.
Get Our Splendid Free Book!
It isn't the kind you can pick up anywhere. Double sized pages, scores of actual photographs—some in full color. Written by an expert on farming. Describes the Ozarks from A to Z and gives actual experiences of men who have gone there. Also gives the best methods of dairying—by an expert on Dairy Husbandry! Worth dollars to any man who farms or expects to. My supply of this book is limited. To be sure of your free copy, fill out this coupon today and mail it to me.
A. HILTON, General Passenger Agent, Frisco Lines, 1524 Frisco Bldg., St. Louis, Mo.
MISSOURI and ARKANSAS
OZARKS
A. HILTON,
Gen'l Pass. Agt.,
Frisco Lines,
1524 Frisco Bldg.,
St. Louis, Mo.
Please send me your free book about the Ozark Country.
Name
Address
FRISCO
LINES
The Heart of the Ozarks
MISSOURI
Kansas City
St. Louis
Springfield
Ft. Smith
Memphis
ARKANSAS

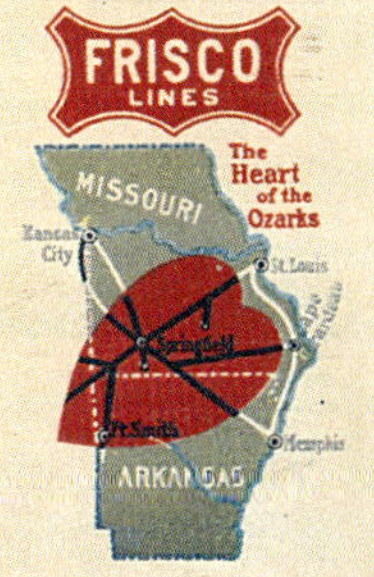

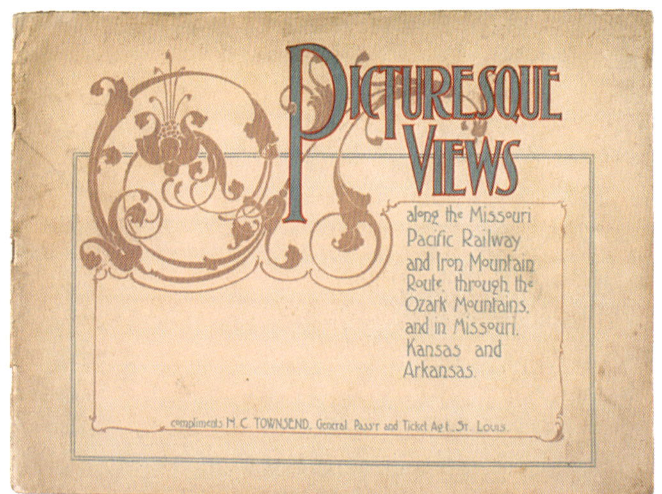

In *Picturesque Views* (left), put out in 1900 by the Iron Mountain Route of the Missouri Pacific Railroad, scenery and recreation are pictured, as well as economic opportunities. The 1930 railroad ad (right) also lauds the beauty of the region and its recreational possibilities. Conflict between economic exploitation and scenic values was apparently unrealized or ignored.

American railroads ran on oak ties harvested from Ozark forests. Tie hacking was a major source of cash for struggling farmers.

Throughout much of its history, the Ozarks had been in a state of arrested economic development. The difficult terrain retarded road-building. Timbering and mining were boom-and-bust activities. Agricultural possibilities were limited.

In the decades after the Civil War, many energetic but under-capitalized folks came to find a better life in the hard-scrabble Ozarks. Many were lured here by advertising put out by the railroads, which were trying to sell parcels of the vast lands they had been given by the government as encouragement to invest in the westward expansion.

Along the railroad lines, towns were platted. On small general farms and in villages, many Americans grew up who were optimistic, God-fearing, and hard working. The post-Civil War, railroad-delivered settlers blended (but not always seamlessly) with those pioneers of Scotch-Irish ancestry who had come into the free-range Ozarks before the Civil War.

Today's native Ozarker is a singularly self-reliant and patriotic American, but suspicious of big government's promises. This profoundly Jeffersonian rurality is part and parcel of the Ozarks' touristic reputation.

In small Ozark towns, as in other parts of rural America, there was a certain antipathy toward sensationalist mass media and the more vulgar forms of urban entertainment. Parades and fairs were, and still are, exceedingly popular. Countless bluegrass and country music festivals, and agricultural and craft fairs held today are put on by and for locals. Tourists who seek out those local affairs are, of course, welcome. Often, they are amazed by how much fun they have.

Long after it vanished elsewhere, that old-time variety show, the tented, traveling Chautauqua, persisted in the Ozarks. The flavor of Ozarkers' taste in entertainment and belief in the democratic community is captured in this program of a 1929 Chautauqua that played in Conway, Arkansas.

Chautauqua was promoted as "fine, fine fun with a friendly picnic atmosphere for the whole community." One evening's program consisted of "cowboy costumes, cowboy range songs, jazz band, accordion, banjo – even cowboy tumbling." On other nights were bits of Broadway plays and Swiss yodelers.

The program stressed the democratic nature of its entertainment and its wholesome character.

Most of us rush through life without stopping for the fine old sociability that our grandfathers enjoyed. The most glorious thing about Chautauqua is the opportunity it gives for the whole neighborhood to take a few days off to laugh at the same jokes, get a thrill from the same inspiring speakers, hear the same great music. It provides a common bond of interest and conversation. Men and women and boys and girls, business men and farmers, Catholic and Protestant, Republicans and Democrats, can all meet at the big tent with no separating influence. It belongs to the whole community.

Midwesterners, as a rule, are far more interested in the outside

world than the outside world is in them—especially if those outsiders are musically talented foreigners, with or without colorful

fiddler, is one of Branson's most popular entertainers. Descendants of Chautauqua's Swiss yodelers may perform at Silver Dollar City's springtime opening event. World Fest brings entertainers and craftsmen from more than 40 countries every year to celebrate spring. The preference for "good clean family variety entertainment" has never gone out of date in the Ozarks.

native costume. Branson's shows and attractions today continue to reflect this curiosity. Shoji Tabuchi, a tuxedo-clad Japanese

The representation of the area as a kind of virtual frontier has at times been exaggerated by the tourist industry. Ozark natives, however, are as keenly interested in the survival of bygone ways as visitors, which this snapshot (above) from a 1940s parade in Cabool illustrates.

LATEST PLAY HITS

"White Collars"

A great play filled with uproarious comedy, clean and wholesome throughout and one that has achieved remarkable success in New York. It is the story of a wealthy man who marries into a family in very moderate circumstances. He attempts to live as his wife has been accustomed to live and almost gives away his entire fortune. Clever comedy throughout the three acts makes "White Collars" a play that will be remembered. It is so true to life, so full of human interest that it absorbes the attention of an audience every minute of the time. There is just enough drama to make it one of the outstanding plays ever put on a Chautauqua circuit.

It has so many tense moments, such clever wit and splendid acting through it all that one will carry away a great lesson and the memory of two hours of real fun.

BROADWAY 1929

Lucile Elmore---Marimba Band

Lucille Elmore, the charming, dainty and diminutive star from the original Broadway cast of "Stepping Stones", which New York audiences paid $5.50 a seat to see, has been secured to bring her Marimba band to Chautauqua patrons. Miss Elmore was starred in Fred Stone's musical comedy success for two years. She is the exponent of modern music and a clean cut brand of entertainment. Her program is a riot of color and melody. Charming and gracious in her manner, Miss Elmore endears herself to any audience.

The Marimba Band is an unique organization. Each member a soloist and composed of some of the most famous marimbaphone players in the country. Miss Elmore and her company will appear both afternoon and evening at Chautauqua with an up-to-the-minute type of 1929 entertainment that will make the closing of Chautauqua a gala event.

CAPTIVATING MUSIC

The Lombards

Seldom does one have the opportunity of seeing and hearing as interesting and entertaining a program as that given by the Lombards. They are well known to radio and theater audiences in the large cities. Harry Lombard has achieved remarkable success as a comedian and musician. Beautiful costumes and stage settings add to the pleasure of the program.

The Masseys of New Mexico

Down in the Southwest when music and musicians are spoken of the Masseys are always mentioned. They are an interesting musical company who have been together for several years and do a wide variety of numbers and do them well. They all sing and play various instruments. Dad Massey is a champion "Old Time Fiddler" but he will also surprise his audience with difficult violin numbers. Their program might be classed as a revue, inasmuch as they give such a varied group of numbers. They are well known all over the United States and Canada.

Fiechtl's Yodeling Tyroleans

Recognized as the foremost company of yodlers in America, Fiechtl's Yodeling Tyroleans will bring Chautauqua goers a program that will stand out as one of the bright spots of the week's festivities. Singing and playing, gaily costumed in the picturesque costumes of the Alpine Mountaineers, they have been a sensation wherever they have appeared. The Fiechtls are all Victor recording artists. Jost and Wunderle have been featured as Zither players by the Victor company.

PLAYGROUNDS OF THE MIDDLE WEST

Rhapsodic invitations from an early 1920s guidebook, published by the Ozark Playgrounds Association, brought a great many American families to see the Ozarks.

The Ozark Mountains are calling you — you as a seeker of invigorating, re-creating and health-building recreations and sport. The Ozarks are calling you to come and play in America's Playgrounds, "The Land of a Million Smiles." This region and its people bid you spend a vacation in a different, joyful way, to bring back those wonderful days of youth. For an Ozark vacation does offer more, more of the real and human features, than other resort districts can give. There is a magnetic touch of something – perhaps it is Mother Nature – which returns thousands of men, women and children to the city, the town or the farm with a cleaner, brighter and happier view of life and its purposes. An Ozark vacation tends to rinse out the dross, erase worries and cares, and paint pictures of brighter hues for the future.

Started in Joplin in 1919 to serve only one section of the region – southwest Missouri, northwest Arkansas, and a sliver of eastern Oklahoma – the Ozark Playgrounds Association became a model of touristic promotion.

Americans' love affair with the auto set in motion a number of new economic opportunities. Road and bridge building,

TOURIST CAMP BRANSON, MO.

The Ozark Playgrounds Association was headquartered in a log cabin in Joplin, Missouri.

car repairs, and the gas business were growth industries. The earliest auto tourists often camped out around rustic shelters, as shown in a rare, real photo postcard (previous page) of a scene near Branson. Soon cabins, lodges, and motels were built to provide greater roadside comfort.

Small-town businessmen saw economic opportunity in providing improved goods and services for tourists. The Playgrounds

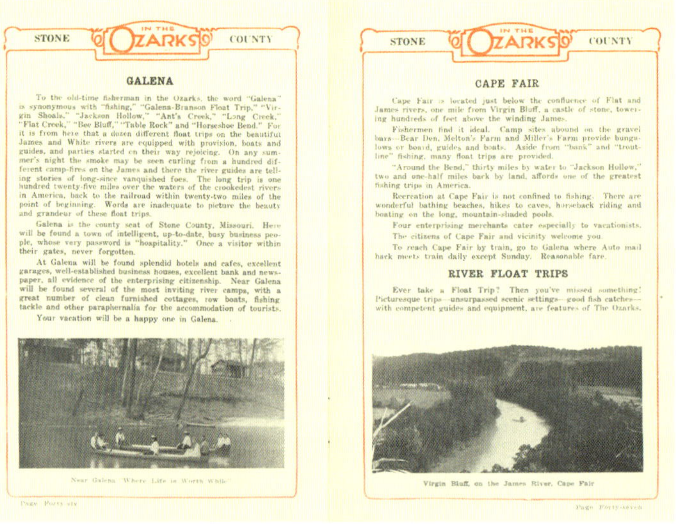

STONE IN THE OZARKS COUNTY

GALENA

To the old-time fisherman in the Ozarks, the word "Galena" is synonymous with "fishing," "Galena-Branson Float Trip," "Virgin Shoals," "Jackson Hollow," "Ant's Creek," "Long Creek," "Flat Creek," "Bee Bluff," "Table Rock" and "Horseshoe Bend." For it is from here that a dozen different float trips on the beautiful James and White rivers are equipped with provision, boats and guides, and parties started on their way rejoicing. On any summer's night the smoke may be seen curling from a hundred different camp-fires on the James and there the river guides are telling stories of long-since vanquished foes. The long trip is one hundred twenty-five miles over the waters of the crookedest rivers in America, back to the railroad within twenty-two miles of the point of beginning. Words are inadequate to picture the beauty and grandeur of these float trips.

Galena is the county seat of Stone County, Missouri. Here will be found a town of intelligent, up-to-date, busy business people, whose very password is "hospitality." Once a visitor within their gates, never forgotten.

At Galena will be found splendid hotels and cafes, excellent garages, well-established business houses, excellent bank and newspaper, all evidence of the enterprising citizenship. Near Galena will be found several of the most inviting river camps, with a great number of clean furnished cottages, row boats, fishing tackle and other paraphernalia for the accommodation of tourists.

Your vacation will be a happy one in Galena.

Near Galena "Where Life is Worth While"

Page Forty-six

STONE IN THE OZARKS COUNTY

CAPE FAIR

Cape Fair is located just below the confluence of Flat and James rivers, one mile from Virgin Bluff, a castle of stone, towering hundreds of feet above the winding James.

Fishermen find it ideal. Camp sites abound on the gravel bars—Bear Den, Melton's Farm and Miller's Farm provide bungalows or board, guides and boats. Aside from "bank" and "troutline" fishing, many float trips are provided.

"Around the Bend," thirty miles by water to "Jackson Hollow," two and one-half miles back by land, affords one of the greatest fishing trips in America.

Recreation at Cape Fair is not confined to fishing. There are wonderful bathing beaches, hikes to caves, horseback riding and boating on the long, mountain-shaded pools.

Four enterprising merchants cater especially to vacationists.

The citizens of Cape Fair and vicinity welcome you.

To reach Cape Fair by train, go to Galena where Auto mail hack meets train daily except Sunday. Reasonable fare.

RIVER FLOAT TRIPS

Ever take a Float Trip? Then you've missed something! Picturesque trips—unsurpassed scenic settings—good fish catches—with competent guides and equipment, are features of The Ozarks.

Virgin Bluff, on the James River, Cape Fair

Page Forty-seven

Association aimed its advertising primarily at middle-class, middle-west, and southern family auto travelers. Its annual guides artistically presented these services to a growing, touring public.

The Ozark Playgrounds Association brilliantly grasped the community-wide economic benefits of tourism. Towns were featured, not just select businesses or attractions. All kinds of opportunities were included in the Association's guides.

Agriculture and retirement development were touted, as well as fishing and sightseeing. The region wasn't just to visit — it was a good place to live and make a living in, as well.

The target audience of the Playgrounds Association was apprehensive about then-fashionable urban Jazz Age decadence. Ozark tourists were nostalgic for the kind of outdoor recreation typical of pre-World War I America. A 1920s Association guidebook emphasizes this continuing interest in swimming, boating, camping, horseback riding, hiking, hunting, and fishing.

"What are your recreation features?" is the first question asked by the man or woman who never has enjoyed a vacation in the Ozarks.

"A life in the out-of-doors" is the logical answer, even though a trifle indefinite and with no mention of the many sports and pleasures which appeal to the average tourist. But it is the life out-of-doors which strikes deepest, even though the Ozark vacation be spent in a resort hotel, cottage, cabin or tent. For the presence and call of Nature in all her wonders reaches through man-made walls and carries them as "trusty" prisoners into the open for fifteen hours of every day. The out-of-doors appeal is irresistible from the very entrance into "The Land of a Million Smiles."

The OZARKS
A glimpse into THE PLAYGROUNDS OF AMERICA
"The land of a million smiles"

The OZARKS
The Land of a Million Smiles

The OZARKS
"The Land of a Million Smiles"

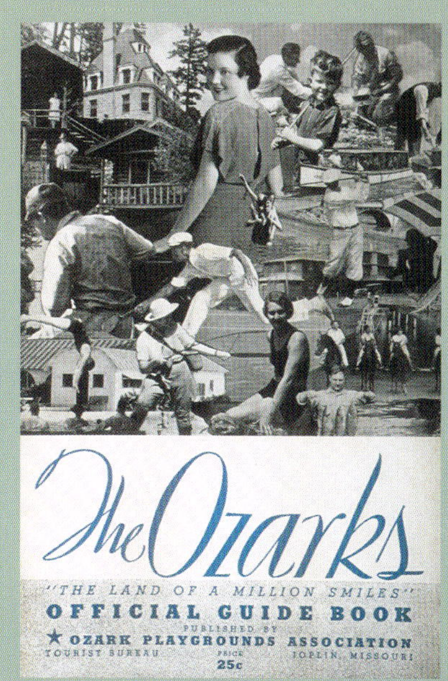

The Ozarks
"THE LAND OF A MILLION SMILES"
OFFICIAL GUIDE BOOK
PUBLISHED BY
OZARK PLAYGROUNDS ASSOCIATION
TOURIST BUREAU
PRICE 25¢
JOPLIN, MISSOURI

The OZARKS
"The Land of a Million Smiles"

Playgrounds of the OZARKS

Let's Go to the...
Playgrounds of the Ozarks
MISSOURI
ARKANSAS
OKLAHOMA
Official Travel Guide of
THE OZARK PLAYGROUNDS ASSOCIATION
EXECUTIVE OFFICES JOPLIN, MISSOURI

OZARK PLAYGROUNDS
The Brightest Star
in Your Vacation Sky
Castle Courts
Fayetteville, Ark.
OFFICIAL GUIDE BOOK

In spite of the hilly nature of the country, road-building made many once-remote areas accessible to the automobile in the 1920s and '30s.

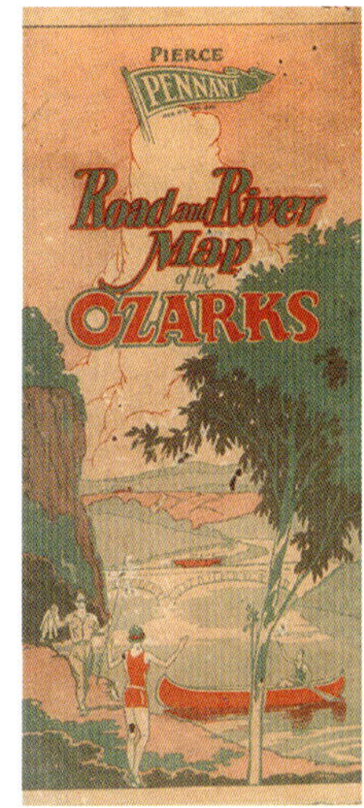

The Ozark roads, although not all of them are yet ideal motor highways, have enjoyed a big improvement within the last two years and many pleasing surprises in roadways will await the motor tourist. An asset is that rain does not make them dangerous or impassable as a result of the natural gravel and sand base. Muddy roads are seldom found throughout the many Ozark counties.

Modern bridges replaced fords, although crossing the headwaters of streams on concrete slabs was still common. Oil companies issued maps that targeted tourists showing these new roads. Postcards celebrated the new travel opportunities. Many portrayed the scenic beauty of the Ozarks, as well as the technical excellence of the improvements.

Pierce Pennant, a St. Louis-based oil company, was an enthusiastic promoter of the Ozarks. Acknowledging that the region exceeded 60,000 square miles, the Pierce map stated that "to mention all resorts, their facilities, attractions, and surrounding

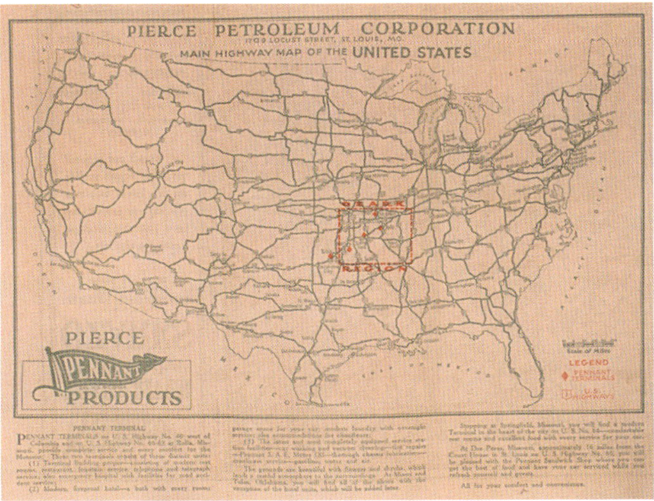

picturesque phenomena would fill an encyclopedia."

U.S. Highway 66 cut across the northern flank of the region. "The Main Street of America" made many Ozarks attractions accessible to auto travelers. As this 1940s Will Rogers Highway (Route 66) luggage sticker indicates, the Ozarks was becoming a national tourist destination on a par with the Grand Canyon, Boulder Dam, and Hollywood. Tourists from the Midwest and beyond access the region today on Interstate 44, which follows the path of old Route 66.

FRISCO
LINES
Vacations
in the
Ozarks

STREAMLINED
DIESEL-POWERED
OZARK STATE
Zephyr
KANSAS CITY
ST. LOUIS
Alton Burlington
BUILT OF STAINLESS STEEL

FRISCO
LINES
FRISCO LINES
112 WEST ADAMS STREET
CHICAGO, ILL.
A PIONEER that
fearlessly cuts its
way through the
gloom of primitive
forests; marches
magnificently
through moun-
tains; courageous-
ly crosses rivers of
destiny; and quiet-
ly builds empires
—The Railroad!

Any way you travel...
OMAHA • DES MOINES • KANSAS CITY • CHICAGO • ST. LOUIS
TOPEKA
WICHITA
LITTLE ROCK
MEMPHIS
THE PLAYGROUNDS OF THE OZARKS
OKLAHOMA CITY • FT. WORTH • DALLAS • SHREVEPORT • NEW ORLEANS
Good Railroads, Highways and Airlines lead to
"THE PLAYGROUNDS of the OZARKS"

Rail tourism was in decline in 1931 when the Frisco Line produced this handsome booklet (opposite page). As roads improved and automobiles became more reliable, vacationers lit out to see the Ozarks. Earlier train-delivered visitors had stayed longer in one place. A boom in roadside businesses that served the auto traveler began.

The Ozarks was promoted by major corporations like Ford as an ideal place to travel in your shiny, new coupe convertible. The Ozark Corporation of Detroit (with factory in West Helena, Arkansas) advertised its 1936 streamlined travel trailers in a jazzy brochure. The American urge to explore is reflected in its ad copy:

You awaken next morning, eager for the call of the open road with its fresh air, bright sunshine, ever-changing beautiful natural scenery, zest of fast travel, and adventure of new things and new country. After all, isn't that living at its best?

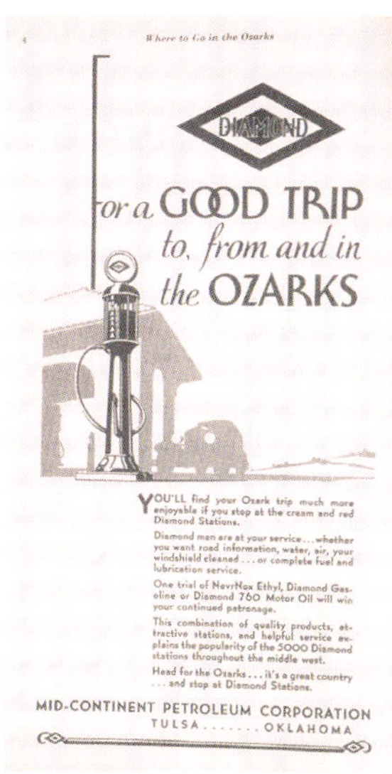

Ford News

IN THE OZARK COUNTRY

B 13608

AUGUST 1933

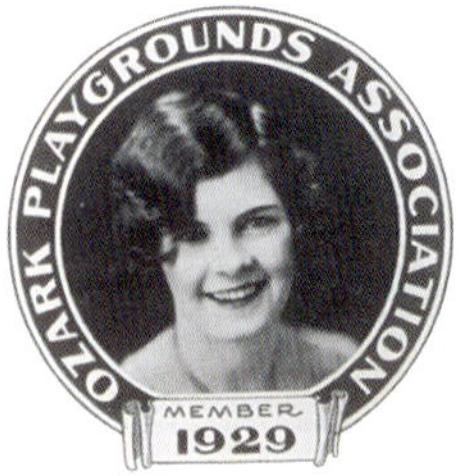

THE OZARK SMILE GIRL

Play in the Ozarks – this year above all others! Significant words, those – and filled with much meaning, for aside from the rare beauty of the scenery, the Ozarks have a direct economic appeal – an outing with little expense, not much more than would be incurred should your vacation be spent at home.

YOUR VACATION IN THE OZARKS

WHATEVER form of recreation may be fancied can be found in the Ozarks. Nature has been lavish in creating delights for pleasure seekers, and Man has added his touch of comfort and convenience wherever one may go. ¶ If it be WATER SPORTS, the places are here in profusion. ¶ If it is CAMPING in the open, then there are endless places for that. ¶ GOLF courses dot the whole Ozark region. ¶ TENNIS may be indulged in here and there. Hiking and climbing wherever you go. HORSEBACK RIDING provided in numerous places. ¶ FISHING wherever there is a place to cast, and that is 'most everywhere. ¶ CANOEING in endless lakes and streams. ¶ MOTOR BOATING in some localities. ¶ PICNICKING places along every mile of highway. ¶ MOTORING is a joy over hundreds of miles of wonderful highways. ¶ HUNTING in season attracts thousands of sportsmen. ¶ BOY SCOUT camps are maintained in many places. ¶ SUMMER HOTELS and dancing. Everything recreational may be found in the Ozarks. ¶ In considering "where to go" this season just remember that "YOU CAN'T GO WRONG IN THE OZARKS"

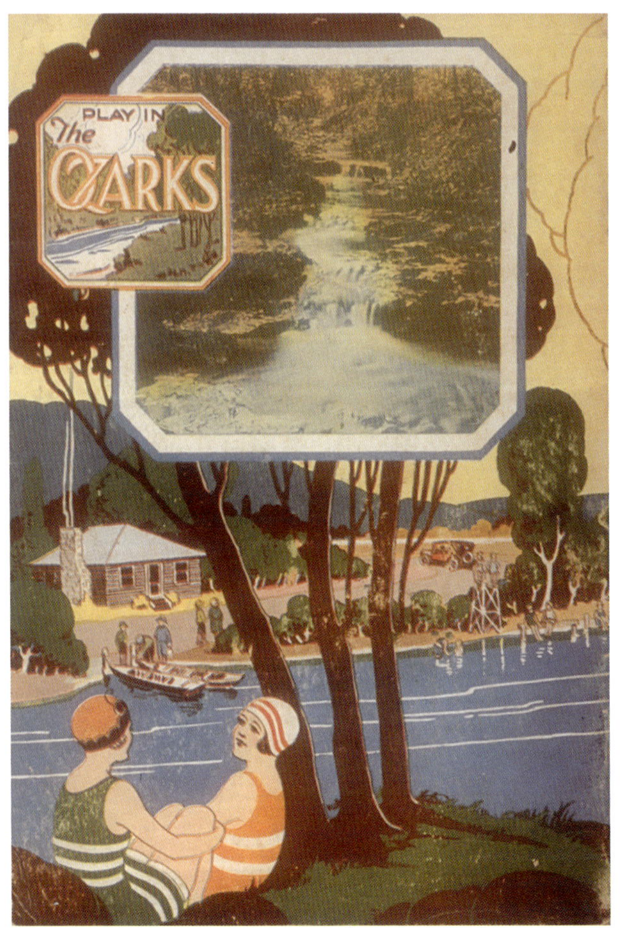

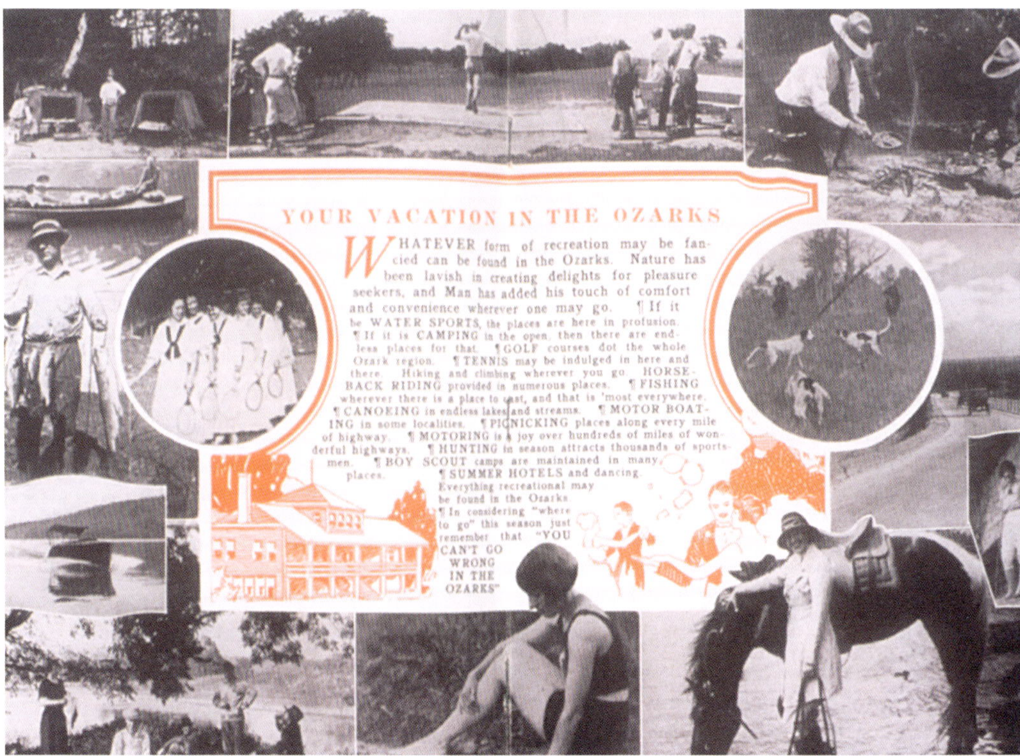

The graphics and design of 1920s and '30s Playgrounds Association pamphlets were less anachronistic than the late Victorian ad copy.

Rusticity remained a central motif in Ozark tourist promotion. As the nation became more industrialized and urban, rural nostalgia became interwoven with the earlier call of the wild that sportsmen had answered. Playgrounds Association phrases like "Land of a Million Smiles" were an invitation to many Americans troubled by the woes of the Great Depression to come see the Ozarks.

The new-fangled ways and modern fashions of city tourists did not always meet with the approval of traditional Ozarkers. Flapper-era swimsuits could cause a raised eyebrow.

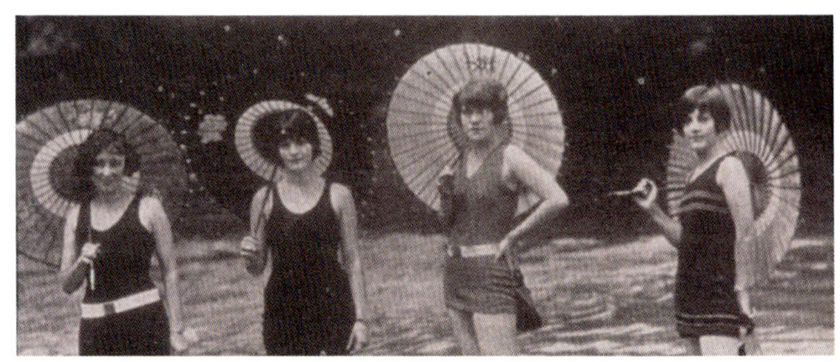

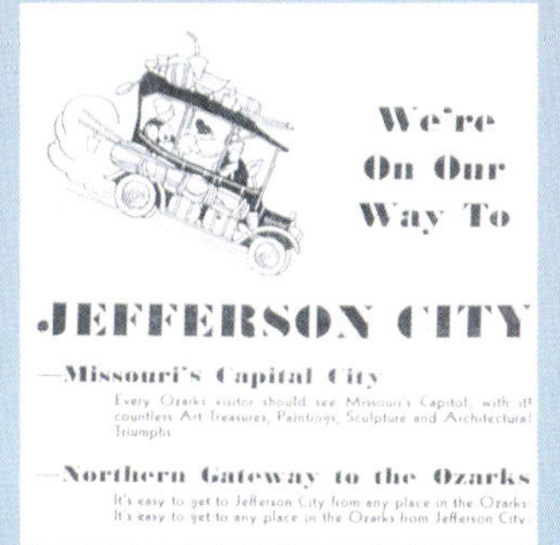

The Ozark Playgrounds Association was an early and innovative marketer of travel and recreation. Other groups advanced the cause, as well. Throughout America, businessmen and civic organizations were enthusiastic believers in the economic benefits of auto tourism.

St. Louis, Kansas City, and Tulsa advertised their proximity to the wondrous Ozarks. Dozens of towns and villages claimed to be the "gateway" to this or that attraction. Local purveyors of gas, food, lodging, beer, soda pop, bait and tackle eagerly sought tourist dollars. More than one chamber of commerce borrowed the Joplin-based group's slogans, "Land of a Million Smiles" or "Playgrounds of the Middle West." Springfield, Missouri was strategically located to profit from the new tourist trade. A rail- and highway-hub, the "Queen City of the Ozarks" had vigorously promoted the region since the early 1900s.

Springfield in the Heart of the Ozarks: in the Land of Ten Thousand Springs welcomes the Fisherman and Vacationist. All highways from Springfield are Roads to Romance that follow sinuous ridges or lead into lonely valleys wherein wind crystal rivers. The Vacationist may fill each day of a long glorious summer with exploration of keenest interest, adventuring forth in the morning and returning to Springfield at evening – tide.

– 1930s Springfield Chamber of Commerce pamphlet

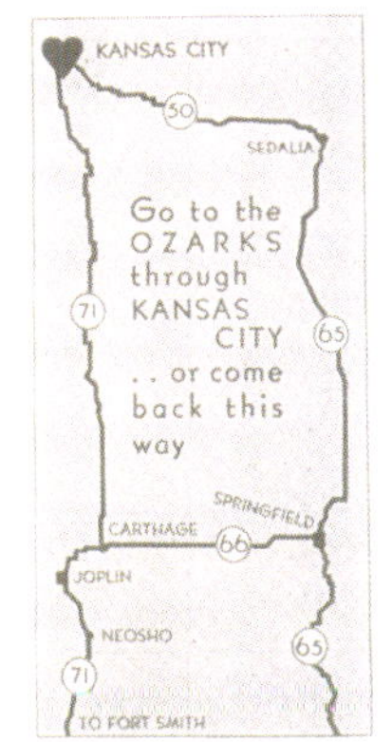

MOUNTAIN TERRACE COURT, US 54, ½ mile W of Bagnell Dam, Lake Ozark, Mo.

Lodges of the early train era were of rustic log construction. Gas stations, restaurants, and motels along the new highways were often faced with slabs of native sandstone. Today called "giraffe stone," these structures were not only eye-catching but were thought to be fireproof. Houses of this construction are still occupied today, while commercial uses are less common. They are either located on bypassed roads or are too petite for modern use.

Variations of this 1930s and '40s vernacular rock architecture use chert rubble as facing.

Enterprises and organizations that generated advertising were rare in Arkansas's Boston Mountains. An uncommonly wild and beautiful area, it was relatively undeveloped due to its rugged topography.

From knobs (as locals call the peaks) 2,000 to 2,500 feet high, one can survey vast wooded tracts of National Forest through which flow streams edged by heroic bluffs. Within the Boston Mountains is the renowned Buffalo National Scenic Riverway. Canoers come from all over America to savor its awe-inspiring scenery.

Roadside businesses clustered along Highway 71 from Fayetteville to Ft. Smith "banded together to tell the world about the opportunities long hidden in this year-round playground of midwest America". The Boston Mountain Resort Association (BMRA) put out brochures extolling the recreational possibilities. Until the contemporary era of nature and eco-tourism, the area was a semi-wilderness best known by hunters, fishermen, and a sparse population of extraordinarily independent hillfolk.

ONE MILLION ACRES of mountains, and valleys, and hills covered with forest of hardwood and pine. Here and there pioneer hamlets of hill folks. Deer play in the woods.
– 1950s Boston Mountain Resort Association pamphlet

SHEPHERD OF THE HILLS COUNTRY

One member of the Ozark Playgrounds Association was destined to mature into a major touristic mecca. The Frisco Railroad cut through the rugged hills of Stone and Taney counties in 1906, crossing the mighty White River at Branson and connecting a virtual frontier with the outside world. The following year, Harold Bell Wright's novel, *The Shepherd of the Hills,* was published. Set in the environs of Branson, with characters loosely based on local hillfolk, the backwoods morality tale struck a resounding chord with audiences nationwide. The bucolic novel quickly became a best seller. Fans of the book rode the newly opened White River Line into Branson seeking the places and people Wright had described in the novel. A tourist industry was founded.

There came one day to this story-laden country a young preacher who pitched his tent in a hillside corn patch of a mountaineer and began to weave into a book the stories his neighbors told him. The man was Harold Bell Wright, the novel was "The Shepherd of the Hills" and the writing of it made the country preacher a millionaire. To the scene of this romance hundreds of people journey each year. The country may be seen exactly as the author described it.

The early 1920s Frisco railroad booklet (left) describes the pilgrim's trip from Branson and Hollister to Inspiration Point

SHEPHERD OF HILLS COUNTRY
TAXI
HOLLISTER
FORSYTHE
REED SPRINGS
AURORA
GALENA
47-986

"seated in hacks drawn by sinewy mountain horses." That trail is now Missouri Highway 76, also called 76 Country Boulevard, the neon-emblazoned Branson "Strip."

Myths can be advertised but not created solely out of the desires of promoters to attract tourists. This area had all of the other Ozarkian recreational opportunities, as well as being the setting for the wildly successful novel. A self-perpetuating publicity machine began to attract recreationalists and tourists from all over America to "The Shepherd of the Hills Country."

By the late 1920s, a tourist-carrying taxi, (previous page) driven by Pearl Spurlock, rattled along that rocky, unimproved road. She related the legends of the region and told hillbilly jokes as she guided adventurous tourists over the hills. "Sparkie," as she was known, was a large woman with unlimited enthusiasm for everything Ozarkian.

Many of Wright's homey melodramas were made

into movies. *The Shepherd of the Hills*, in fact, has been remade several times since the author produced the first version in 1919.

It also made the locals into celebrities. Wright acknowledged only one character as being drawn from life ("Uncle Ike" modeled on Levi Morrill). Nevertheless, many locals claimed to be the inspiration for characters in the novel and posed for postcards.

Sammy Lane on Sammy's Lookout, Shepherd of the Hills, near Lake Taneycomo

Above – H.B. Wright at the set of a 1920s re-make.

Uncle Ike (Levi Morrill) with cave guide and mail carrier Fannabelle Ford Nickel at the Notch Post Office. Sherry, Fannabelle's daughter, married Jack Herschend. Jack, his brother Pete, and their parents, Hugo and Mary, developed Marvel Cave and created Silver Dollar City. (Photo courtesy Sherry Herschend)

Old Matt's and Aunt Molly's log house became a tourist draw soon after the novel was published. The old log cabin is an often-reproduced souvenir and icon of The Shepherd of the Hills Country.

John Wayne starred in the 1941 Technicolor re-make of *The Shepherd of the Hills*. The plot was substantially changed and it was filmed out West.

When built, Taneycomo was a warm water lake, known for its bass, crappie, and occasional big ol' flathead catfish. Today, it is a trout pond, cooled by the deep-water releases from Table Rock Dam.

Recreation in the Shepherd of the Hills Country was enhanced with the creation, in 1913, of a 2,000 acre lake behind a privately built hydropower dam on the White River, 25 river-miles below Branson. Small in comparison to the government-built multi-purpose dams and reservoirs of the 1940s on, Lake Taneycomo (a contraction of Taney County, MO) was poetically described in the copy of an early White River Country railroad brochure.

The lake is wonderful in the morning as the dawn-tints flush the sky, and the sun, outlined faintly as in a Japa-nese etching, peeps from pearl-and-opal mists. In the full splendor of day the sheet of water is gloriously alive with human sights and sounds. Healthy, happy people paddle by in canoes, navigate in motor boats, steam launches and sailboats, and fish for bass and catfish.

A page later, the pamphlet becomes more practical. Mystical delights were even more wonderful when combined with certain modern conveniences. Tourists, it seems, like nature and the great outdoors, but in measured amounts.

The opening of the lake and the consequent opportunities for cheap electric power has brought a contagion of prog-ress to the vacation resort in the mountains. To the primeval beauty of the region it brings twentieth century modernity. It means electric cars, electric-lighted summer hotels, elec-tric conveniences of all kinds. The thrill of the new devel-opment is everywhere. New hotels are going up. Fishing and hunting clubs have incorporated and commenced plans for handsome clubhouses. Bungalows, lodges and camps are building. Enthusiastic good roads boosters are working on a system of automobile roads to connect the charming resorts of this region with the larger cities.

Hotel Rockaway, Rockaway Beach, Lake Taneycomo, Missouri

boarded the Sammy Lane Boat Line for the 20-mile cruise down the lake to the resort. In the evenings, dance bands played on pavilions floating on the lake. Daytime activities included tennis and swimming as well as fishing or touring the sites of Shepherd of the Hills Country. Brochures touted the multitude of available modern services:

Rockaway Beach has four hotels, nearly 250 cottages, general stores (and) gift shop, filling stations, barber shop, beauty parlor, tourist supply and curio store, passenger and outboard motor lines.

The building of Powersite Dam ushered in an era of summer camps and leisure resorts. Chief among them was Rockaway Beach, named after the New York resort town by its developers, Willard and Anna Merriam. Its concept and architecture mirrored the artful rusticity of the Adirondacks style still popular in the East. Not only did the small lake provide pleasure boating opportunities, it generated power for electricity for this out-of-the-way hamlet.

Rockaway became a stylish vacation destination of the teens and twenties. Guests arrived by train at Branson or Hollister and

SWIMMING AT ROCKAWAY BEACH, TANEYCOMO, MO.

This "handprinted in the Ozarks" tablecloth by Branson artist Steve Miller maps the attractions of the Shepherd of the Hills Country in the 1940s. It's a recreational geography of outdoor pleasures – fishing, swimming, boating, caving, exploring, golf, and visiting the sites made famous by Wright's novel.

The region is called Branson or Ozark Mountain Country today. Visitors still have their pictures taken in front of Old Matt's cabin. A stirring pageant based on the book is performed live at Shepherd of the Hills outdoor theater.

In 1960, the closing of Table Rock Dam ended the famous James and White river float trips. Improvements in Highway 65 brought more visitors, but to many it seemed like the end of an era.

On May 1, 1960, a few frontier-type shacks and several restored log cabins were opened to sell refreshments and souvenirs to visitors waiting to tour Marvel Cave. Such was the modest beginning of what would soon be called Silver Dollar City.

The village will as much as possible typify the Ozark Village of Missouri in the late 1800s. Employees within the village will dress in fitting costumes and add to the atmosphere. The Ozark village is not a museum or a ghost town, but a living working village.

– 1959 Marvel Cave press release

In 1950, Hugo and Mary Herschend, a vacationing couple from Chicago, leased Marvel Cave, a tourist attraction since 1896. They loved the Arcadian atmosphere of the Shepherd of the Hills Country. Hugo, a charming and entertaining Danish immigrant, wanted something to do when he retired. Mary had grown up on an Illinois farm and loved the trees and all things Early American. Before his fatal heart attack in 1955, Hugo envisioned a craft village on the property. It would be left to his widow and their sons, Jack and Pete, to fulfill his dream.

Silver Dollar City's version of the Ozark past is popular because it features ordinary people, their daily activities and preferences in food, socialization, and entertainment. As in Harold Bell Wright's novel, the players are farmers, millers, blacksmiths, small-town tradesmen, even a few local rowdies. Like American democracy, everyone has a role, even audience members who are often drawn into the action. Before the term was a buzzword, Silver Dollar City was interactive. The citizens of the city (as the employees are called) share with the mostly middle-American visitors the frontier values of friendliness, honesty, hard work, patriotism, religious values, and a penchant for wisecracking.

Over two million come to the park each year to take in its craft demonstrations, rides, music theaters, country food, and to enjoy its five distinct festivals.

At the junction of highways No. 65 and 86 or the crossroads between Hollister and Tablerock, stands a tall jar of brilliant blue, from beside which one may gaze off to see majestic Dewey Bald shouldering the sky. You may also see many small jars of all sizes and shapes in a very attractive variety of colors to please the many tourists who stop there. This craft known as Como-Craft was originated at this point by Harold Horine.

– Pearl Spurlock

How single-color painted concrete urns and vases evolved into multicolor drip pottery is not known. This colorful species of roadside souvenir ware currently enjoys considerable cachet among collectors. The photo above was published in a 1943 *National Geographic* article on the Ozarks. Unfortunately, it is not identified except the location is Hollister.

You will see the natives all along the highways weaving baskets. This is a very pleasant as well as profitable work, as they sell enough to the tourists, or "furners" as they say, to help them live a "right smart while". The baskets are made in various shapes and sizes, and mostly of white oak.

– Pearl Spurlock

Distinctive souvenirs were produced in the Shepherd of the Hills Country and sold at roadside curio and gift shops, like Chula Vista. The shops were stocked with locally made baskets and pottery, and chenille spreads brought in from the southeastern United States. Some of those inexpensive souvenirs now fetch many times their original price.

Vacationers, like Hugo and Mary Herschend, who leased Marvel Cave in 1950, found these handmade items worthy mementos of their sojourn in the hills. Hugo Herschend's early vision was to bring together local craftsmen to show visitors the objects being made. Silver Dollar City developed in large part from this idea.

HILLFOLK AND HILLBILLIES

Much ink, and a little blood, has been spilled over classifying the natives of the Ozarks. Though the term "hillbilly" did not appear in print until 1900, early educated travelers found the character of the southern mountaineer a tad raw, but raw material for literature, nevertheless.

When tourists found backwoods Ozarkers' anachronistic lifestyle quaint, even reminiscent of our pioneer ancestors, they were deemed "hillfolk." When locals resisted development, such as dams and highways or were disinterested in changing a vacationer's flat tire in the rain, they were "hillbillies."

In the 1930s and 1940s, hillbilly-ness was hot. Some of this was jokey, even demeaning, but many of the portraits of rural rubes were good-hearted. The audience for such fare brought with it a collective recent memory of rural poverty and the life-

The Weaver Brothers and Elviry were native Ozarkers whose hillbilly light comedy was successful on the vaudeville stage and in movies. Their "Hill-Billy Review" (right) is shown in this 1930s press photo.

Theatrical
chiCAGO

In the Ozarks nearly anywhere you choose to strike, if you venture a little way off of the main-traveled highways, you will find a splendid stock of sturdy American humanity, rare and racy of the soil: last survivors of a hard race of mountaineers, whose virtues and whose vices alike, contrasted with those of the Jazz Age, are refreshing to contemplate.

The real saga of these people never has been written. From the hills of the Carolinas and Virginia the forefathers of the Ozarks' foremost families began trekking westward so long ago as the days just before the Revolution, seeking more elbow room, and finding it in other high land in Kentucky and Tennessee. Onward, next, to the Ozarks of Missouri and Arkansas and Oklahoma.

Here was their last stand, for as hillfolk they 'honed not' for the flat prairies which lay beyond. Rose Wilder Lane, who comes closer to doing justice to this mountain epic, catches the spirit of the old-time Ozark pioneers when in "Hill-Billy" she has one of her characters say: "The lowlands, they raise corn. But 'tis the hills raise men."

–The Ozarks: Highlands of the Middle West, *The Mentor*, 1927

Local color writers have long found hillfolk ideal subject matter. Before improved transportation, mass media, and public education homogenized America, the region's rural inhabitants were seen to be colorfully old fashioned. This hillfolk portrait of poor but proud backwoods Americans became the unintended inspiration for the uninhibited, cartoonish, pop culture hillbilly of the 1930s and '40s.

C. P. Cushing from Galloway

A primitive store of the old days in Ozarkland, at Timberlains Ferry, in Stone County, Missouri. If you wanted to buy something you called the storekeeper in from his fields to serve you

THE OZARKS
The Highlands of the Middle West

THE very word "Ozarks" itself has a romantic sound; implying remoteness, wild and rugged scenery; and to some extent, even to this day, truly primitive conditions of living.

"None can care for literature in itself," Robert Louis Stevenson once shrewdly remarked, "who do not take a special pleasure in the sound of names; and there is no part of the world where nomenclature is so rich, poetical, humorous and picturesque as the United States of America."

You need not go outside of Iron County, Missouri, or stir from this eerie where we have perched for a view-

C. P. Cushing from Galloway

Fifteen years ago: an Ozark settler's mud-chinked log cabin, with rough-hewn shingles and no window glass

point upon the highest tip of old Pilot Knob, or even shift the direction of your sight down the white thread of highway which stretches southward through this inviting valley, to find plentiful instances. Do you seek richness, poetry in names? Then "Arcadia Valley" lies straight ahead, and this is the road to "Sabula," "Vulcan" and "Des Arc." Or do you seek humor? Then keep to the same stretch of highway for "Hogan," "Pippin" and tiniest "Minimum." Picturesqueness next? What better could you ask than "Pilot Knob" itself? Or, turning now toward the west but still not budging outside of the limits

of Iron County, over there lies "Graniteville," and beyond it "the Black River country," with "Tom Sauk," "Viburnum" and "Wildcat Mountain."

So it goes through all this land; nowhere else can you find names more prosy or names more poetical. As in near-by Shannon County, with towns so cursed upon the map as "Ink," "Alley," "Rat," "Sinkin" and "Horse Hollow," or so blessed as "Oakside," "Congo" and "Angeline." Or hark to the roll (is it not like a poem?) which the train conductor calls on the Current River Branch east-bound into Shannon County out of "Mountain View": "Teresita! Monteer! Birch Tree! Winona! Low Wossie!" Then at "Fremont," the next stop, perhaps a traveler debarks for "Barren" or for "Wilderness."

But the best of it all, here in the Ozarks, is the noble way in which the really important centers of tourist attraction, even in these rapidly changing times, live up to the alluringly high promise of their names. For an example near at hand, "Pilot Knob" so truly looks its part that it gets credit for much greater height than it actually attains; many of its neighbors are loftier hills by far. Certainly, no one who clambers to the highest pinnacle of this cone can complain that the panorama here is not of the sort that red-backed guidebooks mark as "*View*." Even Baedeker, who accords the entire Ozark region only two brief mentions, does not grudge to "Arcadia Valley" the distinction of "charming." Iron County in general lives up to all its richness of names. It is not, even today, wholly impossible that a hunter might flush a wildcat upon "Wildcat

C. P. Cushing from Galloway

A GROUP OF OZARK CHILDREN

This was their "Sunday best" not so long ago—ragged calico and broken shoes. Now city styles reach them by mail-order catalogue

Mountain." As for "Graniteville," never was a town christened more conservatively.

All the other really outstanding "high spots" of a well-guided Ozark pilgrimage are equally satisfying. Fare on next, southward, to those rival giants of Ozark springs, "Big" and "Mammoth." Again, for all their large promise, they do not disappoint; they are, in fact, among the world's largest, veritable rivers, boiling up from subterranean depths. The landscapes of the "White River country" also, as you have a right to expect, disclose all the peace and loveliness of the famed valleys of rural England. The Ozarks of "Arkansas" (a name upon which Stevenson did not fail to comment, with a warning to pronounce it "Arkansaw" to get the full poetic flavor) are as rugged and bristling as you might crave to have them. Likewise have such caves as "Marvel" and "Fairy" a right to all that their names connote. And "Hahatonka" is yet as delightful a spot and almost as primitive as when the poetic-minded Indians christened it, because of its great sparkling spring, "Laughing Water." The vista here is one which ought to be world-famous.

As has been hinted in a passing reference to Baedeker, this is a land almost unknown to guidebooks; indeed, until a few years ago it was very nearly "a land that nobody knows." So it may be helpful next to define, roughly, its boundaries.

That breeze which sweeps up to us here on the peak of Pilot Knob from out of the southwest may, for all we know, have borne its high-piled summery clouds from as far away as the most distant westerly limits of the region. It may have rolled up those big style it dictated. European immigrants and transplanted Okies alike had personal experiences — both positive and negative — with impoverished country life, as well Ozarkers. The hillbilly became a classic American stereotype. Ill-educated, musically talented, unintentionally funny, and fabulously indifferent to the disciplines of the workaday world, their corny predicaments delighted audiences across the land. Even in the Great Depression, their antics were worth the price of admission.

Questions aside on the accuracy of journalistic writing at its best, the business of characterizing rural Ozarkers has been controversial. Early local-color writers' descriptions of the old fashioned, but fascinating, lifestyle of hillfolk were fairly realistic, but selective. There were educated, traveled, middle-class types in small towns throughout the region, as well as holdouts from frontier days. To characterize the entire Ozarks as "hillbilly-land" simply wasn't true, but Ozark doctors, lawyers, bankers, and school teachers don't make as good a copy as log-cabin-dwelling, homespun-clad, coon doggers and folk singers.

The bourgeoisie of the county seats (not radical progressives themselves) were as intrigued by the survival of old-time ways as the tourists. Native Ozarkers of all classes were rarely incensed by hillbilly imagery. Even if occasionally cruelly exaggerated, they found it somewhat valid and often amusing. In the bigger towns, hard-core progressives, however, didn't get the joke. The idea that everything wasn't up-to-date in the Ozarks riled them.

As tourism began to look like a money maker in the 1930s, some businessmen feared that the idea that the region was populated by gun-toting moonshiners would scare off potential visitors. John T. Woodruff, hotel owner and driving force in the Springfield, Missouri Chamber of Commerce, was incensed at all aspects of hillbilly-ness.

The typical Ozarkian is no hillbilly at all but a high-minded, patriotic and God-fearing citizen. Never get the idea that is rampant today that they are uncouth, illiterate and mean, and possessed of none of the finer sensibilities.

Woodruff even took aim at Harold Bell Wright's novel, *The Shepherd of the Hills,* saying Wright "hardly knew a thing about the region" and "measured by any standard of a literary man, he couldn't pass the third grade."

Earthy accounts of Ozark rustics made the hotelier apoplectic.

Woodruff pronounced Thames Williamson's novel, *The Woods Colt* (dedicated to Vance Randolph), "the rottenest, nastiest stuff I've ever seen in print."

Vance Randolph – arguably the best writer on the Ozarks ever – differed. He thought – as did most Ozarkers – that the hillfolk/hillbilly concept served touristic interests by giving the region a distinct identity.

The professional Ozark boosters would do well to put more of this primitive stuff into their advertising, and not talk so much about our splendid highways and excellent new hotels. City people won't come down here simply to stop in a shiny new tavern, because there are still plenty of

comfortable hotels in Chicago and St. Louis, even Kansas City. They come to see rugged mountain scenery and quaint log cabins and picturesque rail fences and romantic-looking mountaineers. It is this sort of thing and not mere modern conveniences that pulls the tourist trade. One of Harold Bell Wright's novels got more valuable publicity for the Ozarks than all of the "booster" associations combined, and the Weaver Brothers have brought more tourists into the Ozarks than all of the chambers of commerce in Arkansas.

The Woods Colt (a country term for an illegitimate child) was a 1933 melodrama set in the Ozarks, like the 1907 *The Shepherd of the Hills*. Thames Williamson's emphasis on outlawry, moonshining, sex, and violence was more indicative of the predominant tone of naturalistic novels in the 1930s, than it was of any profound social changes in the Ozarks during the three decades that separated the two works. *The Woods Colt* today is an obscure, forgotten tome in a used book store. Books may contribute to a place's image, but rarely do novels have the touristic impact of *The Shepherd of the Hills*.

The 1930s postcard (above) presumes some realism. The 1940s cartoon treatment of Ozarkers (below) is pure pop culture. However treated, the hillbilly image is emblematic of the Ozarks. Hillbilly motifs decorate a thousand kinds of Ozark souvenirs.

Arkansas has been especially identified with the concept of hillbilly-ness, though most of the state does not lie within the Ozark uplift. Even before the Civil War, *The Arkansas Traveler,* song and story, was distasteful to progressive Arkansans.

Clifton Johnson, in his 1906 book, *Highways and Byways of the Mississippi Valley,* captures that long-standing prejudice.

Among the state's immediate neighbors it is customary to speak slightingly of conditions across the line, and you would gather the impression that life and manners there were rather cruder than anywhere else in the great valley. The outside dwellers take particular pleasure in repeating a curious legend known as "The Arkansaw Traveller." This tale has been a favorite for more than half a century, and, told properly, it has a musical accompaniment. Formerly, whenever there was a social gathering that included a man with a violin, this man was sure to be asked to play "The Arkansaw Traveller"; and the listeners took equal delight in the cheery jig of the music and in the medley of jokes that went with it.

His residence is primitive, his moonshine potent, his gun handy, his daughter fulsome, his hounds lean – and the mountaineer's retorts to the traveler are hilarious. Ever since, the Arkansas hillbilly mythos has been spread by vaudeville acts, records, movies, joke books, postcards, and decals.

In Thomas W. Jackson's 1903 pulp joke book, *On A Slow Train Through Arkansas*, only a few comic pieces are about Arkansas and none specifically mention the Ozarks. Ultimately, the collection of vaudevillian snickers sold three million copies, most hawked on slow trains. *Slow Train...* and Jackson's companion booklet, *Through Missouri On A Mule*, contributed to the public's identification of low humor with mountaineers. The idea that all of Arkansas is, indeed, a hillbilly homeland seems to have a life of its own.

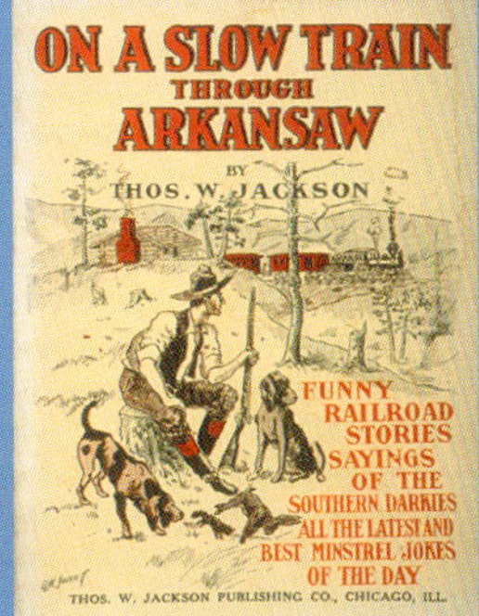

In between making comedies in Hollywood, the Weaver Brothers and (sister) Elvirey, traveled the vaudeville circuit in their bus named "The Arkansas Traveler."

If the Playgrounds Association promoted the region as "The Land of a Million Smiles," Hollywood thought the Ozarks was "The Land of a Million Yucks." "Hick flicks" have had a long history. Early silent films often cast mountaineers as villains. In 1930s and '40s movies, the hillbilly was portrayed as a good-hearted, but poor and uneducated, rube. In spite of such disadvantages, their native wit often helped them best a city slicker out to steal the farm.

Arkansas comic, Bob Burns, cashed in on his Ozarkian wit in radio and movies. In later life, he operated a souvenir shop and motel on Route 71 in the Boston Mountains. His line of hillbilly postcards reflected the sharp, satiric humor characteristic of much Depression- and World War II-era popular culture.

Hillbilly-ness was not confined to the Ozarks. Al Capp, a brilliant social satirist of Jewish ancestry, created *Li'l Abner*, a cartoon hill country universe, in the 1930s and '40s. Capp's artfully drawn cast of maladjusted yahoos was not specifically Ozarkian, but did finally come to rest there.

Dogpatch USA was a touristic venture opened in 1968 just south of Harrison, Arkansas. Li'l Abner, his kith and kin, however, failed to survive transplantation from funny paper to theme park. Factors contributing to its demise were: its out-of-the-way location, the comic strip was no longer carried in newspapers, a television series failed to materialize, and beaucoup business shenanigans. That era also saw increasing national sensitivity to ethnic stereotypes. The place closed in 1993 because of poor attendance.

A few old-timers could still remember handed-down, 300 year-old tunes as improved highways brought tourists and song collectors like Vance Randolph into isolated parts of the Ozarks in the 1920s and '30s . Randolph's published collections of this remarkable survival of folk songs of the British Isles fill several feet of library shelves.

In the late 1800s, sheet music and pianos arrived in small towns by rail. The new roads allowed phonographs and radios to be trucked in. Ozark musical heritage is more diverse than *National Geographic* feature articles or PBS documentaries infer. Folklorish elements are real, but other influences are present. Authenticity is a scholarly concept, not a musical value. In musical matters, as in literature, the hillfolk/hillbilly debate raged on.

The region certainly was settled by a musically inclined people, but their interests continued to evolve and diversify. Echoes of the old, handed-down ballad tradition melded with newer, media-disseminated forms to create commercial country music. Since the 1950s, local groups have been successfully entertaining tourists with what was originally called hillbilly music. Revival bluegrass and folk music are popular at festivals. The Ozark hills are alive with music and the sound of visitors' applause.

May Kennedy McCord (above) had a radio show and newspaper column called *Hillbilly Heartbeats*. The "Queen of Hillbillies" contributed 70 authentic Ozark folk songs to Randolph's books.

Red Foley's mid-1950s *Ozark Jubilee* (right), broadcast live from Springfield on ABC TV, was so successful it looked for a time like the town might become the capital of country music. Forty years later, Branson, 30 miles south, has become the largest live music venue in the U.S. Its offerings are pop as well as country, but local hillbilly variety shows, the Baldknobbers Jamboree and Presley's Country Jubilee, are two of the town's most successful theaters.

The late Lee Mace founded a similar country show, Ozark Opry, at Lake of the Ozarks in the early 1950s. It still packs 'em in.

These fast-paced, colorful shows feature snappy hillbilly humor, alternating with well-performed commercial country music. Popular with tourists, they prove that Ozark culture can be simultaneously traditional and innovative.

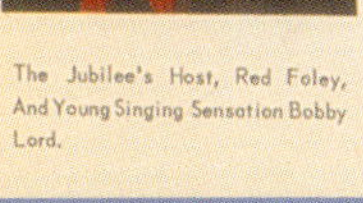

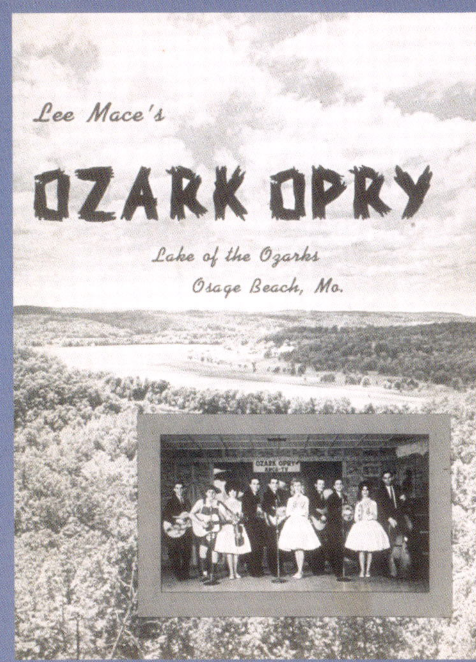

Ozarker Albert E. Brumley Sr. wrote and published country classics like *Turn Your Radio On* and *I'll Fly Away*. Son Tom, renowned pedal steel guitarist, heads a Brumley country music show in Branson.

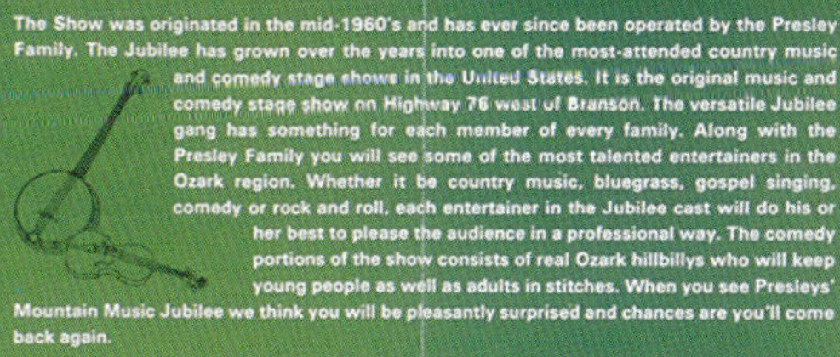
The Show was originated in the mid-1960's and has ever since been operated by the Presley Family. The Jubilee has grown over the years into one of the most-attended country music and comedy stage shows in the United States. It is the original music and comedy stage show on Highway 76 west of Branson. The versatile Jubilee gang has something for each member of every family. Along with the Presley Family you will see some of the most talented entertainers in the Ozark region. Whether it be country music, bluegrass, gospel singing, comedy or rock and roll, each entertainer in the Jubilee cast will do his or her best to please the audience in a professional way. The comedy portions of the show consists of real Ozark hillbillys who will keep young people as well as adults in stitches. When you see Presleys' Mountain Music Jubilee we think you will be pleasantly surprised and chances are you'll come back again.

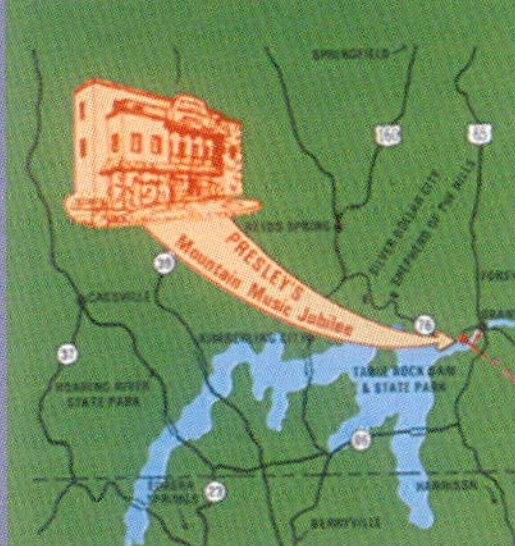

ARCADIANS

Rural nostalgia is a very old story. Even the ancient Greeks longed for a mythic, trouble-free past or an uncorrupted pastoral retreat, which they located in the region of Arcadia. Like the Greeks, writers and philosophers have often associated cities with humanity's cares, and country life with the carefree. Arcadianism is a belief that nature and the natural life are morally superior to, and less vexing than, life in the bustling, artificial city. This romantic outlook ebbs and flows through Western history depending on the stress levels progress imposes.

Ho, to the hills with me, Far from the city's din,
Fleeing its ills with me, Squalor and want and sin.

Those lines from a poem by Reverend William M. Runyan in the *Daily Doings* pamphlet (above) capture the tone of Arcadianism Ozark-style. Put out in 1925 by a real estate and summer camp development of Sulfur Springs, Arkansas, it is hardly revolutionary. Settled by pragmatic pioneers and drawing its tourist trade from the prosaic populace of the Middle West, Ozark culture can rarely be characterized as radical.

As pioneer ways survived in the Ozarks long after they melted

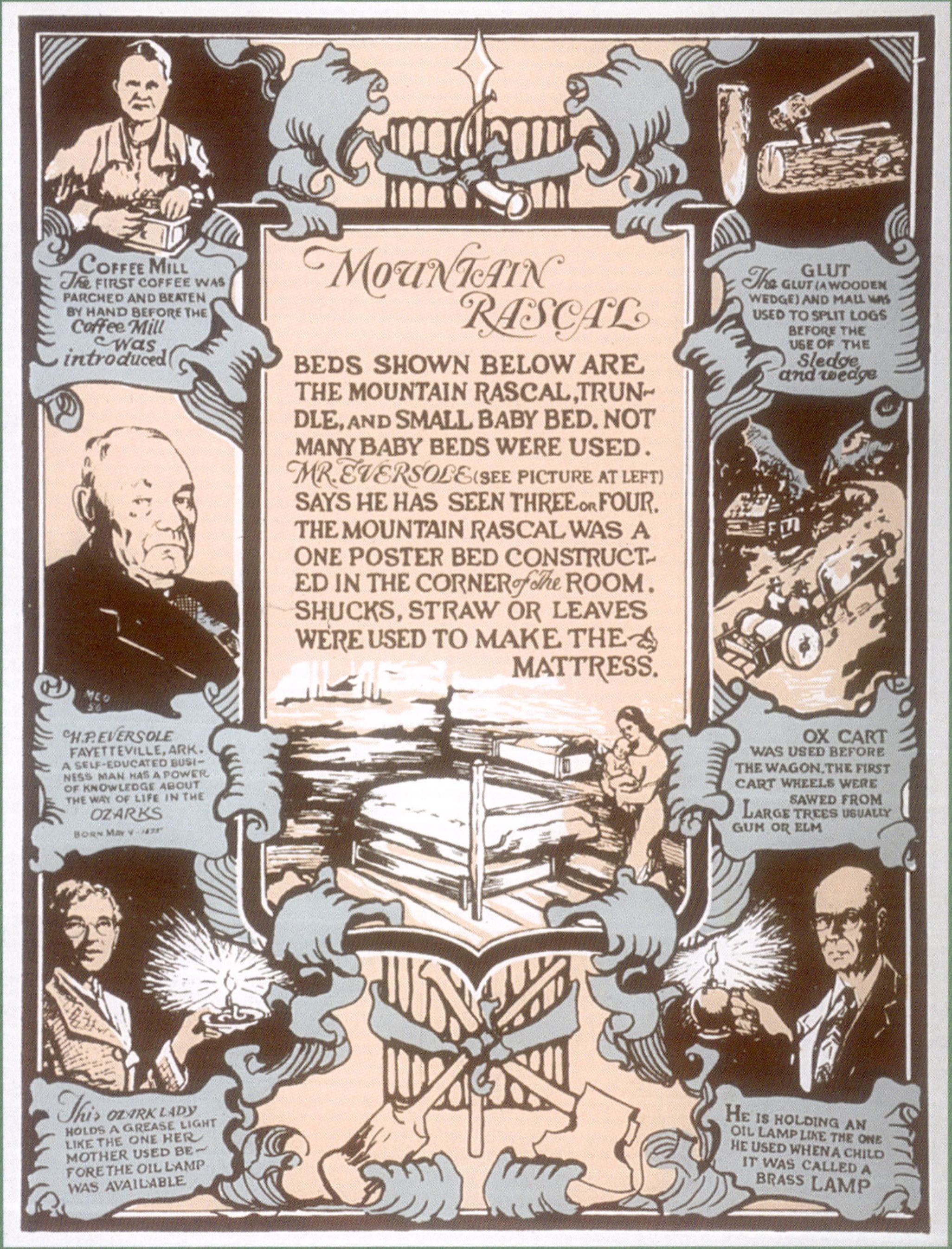

MOUNTAIN RASCAL

BEDS SHOWN BELOW ARE THE MOUNTAIN RASCAL, TRUNDLE, AND SMALL BABY BED. NOT MANY BABY BEDS WERE USED. MR. EVERSOLE (SEE PICTURE AT LEFT) SAYS HE HAS SEEN THREE OR FOUR. THE MOUNTAIN RASCAL WAS A ONE POSTER BED CONSTRUCTED IN THE CORNER OF THE ROOM. SHUCKS, STRAW OR LEAVES WERE USED TO MAKE THE MATTRESS.

COFFEE MILL — The FIRST COFFEE WAS PARCHED AND BEATEN BY HAND BEFORE THE Coffee Mill WAS introduced

GLUT — The GLUT (A WOODEN WEDGE) AND MALL WAS USED TO SPLIT LOGS BEFORE THE USE OF THE Sledge and wedge

H.P. EVERSOLE FAYETTEVILLE, ARK. A SELF-EDUCATED BUSINESS MAN HAS A POWER OF KNOWLEDGE ABOUT THE WAY OF LIFE IN THE OZARKS. BORN MAY 4 - 1875

OX CART WAS USED BEFORE THE WAGON. THE FIRST CART WHEELS WERE SAWED FROM LARGE TREES USUALLY GUM OR ELM

This OZARK LADY HOLDS A GREASE LIGHT LIKE THE ONE HER MOTHER USED BEFORE THE OIL LAMP WAS AVAILABLE

HE IS HOLDING AN OIL LAMP LIKE THE ONE HE USED WHEN A CHILD IT WAS CALLED A BRASS LAMP

The primitive aspects of mountain life were interesting to natives as well as to Arcadians who came into the Ozarks to write about it. Encouraged by the larger world's interest in them, certain talented native Ozarkers portrayed in words and pictures the folklorish aspects of their lives. Among the most gifted was Marvin Elmer Oliver, born in 1888 near Drakes Creek in Arkansas.

Oliver was wounded in World War I. During his rehabilitation, he studied art in New York City. He missed the hills of home so he returned, married, and farmed for a time. Upon retirement, he produced drawings and paintings from his memories of pioneer life and times.

These silk-screened images are a poignant reminder that the Arcadian dream of a harmonious life close to nature is a widely held vision.

into memory elsewhere, Ozark Arcadianism has a particularly old-fashioned style. Even tourist promotion was tinged by anachronistic, romantic literary modes.

Nationwide, pastoral invitations to travel were fading by the 1930s. Still, the Frisco Railroad must have thought such prose would resonate with folks interested in seeing the Ozarks. A 1931 Frisco pamphlet carries on the tradition of poetic promotion more typical of the turn of the century.

Surely all rainbows lead to the Ozarks. This beauteous sylvan region upon which a prodigal nature has lavished her manifold gifts, offers an Arcadian avenue of escape from the everyday world of reality into an enchanted realm of new wonders and delights.

The crash of 1929 threw much that was old hat into question. Intellectuals, trendsetters, and progressive politicians got busy engineering a new Machine Age from the economic and social rubble. Beliefs in nature and agrarian values were dismissed by modernists as irrelevant.

Art deco was not a popular parlor style with the typical Ozark tourist. Aspects of modernism, often associated with urbanism, were disconcerting to many Americans, especially as the Great Depression deepened. Many such culturally conservative folks came to the Ozarks to find some peace of mind and respite from the new world of rapid change.

The region has long been a magnet for dreamers. In the late 1800s, "the world-weary" escaped to Eureka Springs. Disenchantment with modernity was not uncommon after World War I, either. Not all Lost Generation rebels went off to Paris. Some, like Vance Randolph, came to the Ozarks. They expressed their feelings in prose, poetry, and pictures. This rural and rustic literary output colored the popular perception of the region. Not really intended as tourist promotion, Arcadian art and literature communicated that the Ozarks was still a place of natural harmony and traditional culture.

To write mist-on-the-water, romantic poetry, one should ideally observe pristine nature firsthand. Even after a century of exploitation for industrial materials, there remain substantial areas of native forest, clear rivers, and splendid vistas. If not virginal, some of the Ozarks was, and is, wild and beautiful. Much of the rest is suitably bucolic.

The Arcadians' interest in hillfolk culture may seem odd. Early nineteenth century romantic art and books most often painted or depicted an innocent child of nature, like an Indian, in his wilderness landscape. The Ozarkian brand of Arcadianism had to make do with hillbillies, an unlikely primitive hero.

American pioneers of Scotch-Irish origin were scarcely motivated by esthetics. Ax and rifle in hand, they fought the Indians across the Appalachians into the Ozarks. Remnants of seventeenth-century British traits survived in their descendants' habits. Two-hundred-year-old songs and speech patterns and medieval crafts were intriguing to the Arcadians. The old folks who possessed this vanishing culture were no friends of progress, either. They enjoyed, generally, the attention of folklorists, and a coalition of sorts was formed. Sometimes, the locals would write or paint themselves, like M. E. Oliver (opposite page). Believers in the simple Ozarks life were and are numerous, though diverse in outlook and background.

Otto Ernest Rayburn exemplified the somewhat contradictory impulses of Ozark-style Arcadianism. He published a series of small periodicals, one of which was entitled *Arcadian Magazine: A Journal of the Well-Flavored Earth*, centered on Ozark subject matter. The literary business scarcely paid the bills, so he taught school and sold real estate, as well. He would wax poetic:

I find the solitary places of the Ozark hills ideal retreats for capturing the moon's gold and harvesting contentments from simplicity.

Then, in another 1930s issue, Rayburn noted:

I would like to make an extensive study of profanity as used by hillfolk. In the Ozarks we have men who put artistry in their oaths, extracting them with symmetry and rhythm that far outclasses common, ordinary, monotonous swearing.

Such were the Ozark Arcadians: romantics at heart, but with a keen appreciation of the gritty wit and wisdom of fading pioneer folkways.

Tourists are, after all, temporary Arcadians. A vacation Ozark-style often includes some unwinding in a natural setting or relaxation in outdoor sports. For a few travelers to the region, that was not enough. They stayed and wrote, sang, crafted, or painted their vision of an idyllic life in the Ozarks.

Commercial promotion of the Ozarks could at times be indistinguishable from artistic Arcadian publications, as this page from an early 1920s Playgrounds Association pamphlet shows.

BELLA VISTA

In the heart of the famous Land of a Million Smiles. Four miles north of Bentonville, Ark.; sixty-five miles south of Joplin; over splendid scenic auto driveways; follow the black and white markings; eight hours' drive from Tulsa and Muskogee; one day's easy drive from Oklahoma City.

The Ozark's largest, most popular, most diversified, most homelike family, pleasure and summer home resort. One hundred-room hotel, excellent meals and service, family style. Local and long-distance telephones. Two hundred privately-owned summer homes, modern. Electric lights, sewerage, shower baths, beautiful mountain lake stocked with game fish; bathing, rowing. Dancing each week night; music by seven-piece St. Louis orchestra the entire season. Beautiful and interesting nine-hole golf course. Moving pictures, tennis, trapshooting, horseback riding, exploring, hiking, children's playground in natural scenic park, bridge and five-hundred clubs. Many points of historic and scenic interest within few miles over excellent roads.

We welcome you to Bella Vista. Come here to play mid nature's grandeur. Come here to rest and recreate in your own cozy summer home, which we build for you complete. The cost is small. Dividends in good health and rejuvenation to you and your family are big.

Don't go home without coming to Bella Vista. Attractive literature on request. Linebarger Brothers, Owners, Bentonville, Ark.

Fishing at Bella Vista

Bella Vista was an early, successful, upscale Ozark real estate venture. In 1917, the Linebarger brothers, developers of Dallas, Texas bought out a struggling rustic resort in northwest Arkansas. As well as Arcadian outdoor pastimes like horseback riding, swimming, and boating, a dance band played every night but Sunday. The new oil-rich of Oklahoma and Texas, including Osage Indians and Will Rogers, built fine summer homes here. A pioneer in developing vacation and retirement homes, Bella Vista still thrives.

Once a lot was purchased, one could use the resort's extensive amenities and attend the special events: fireworks, air shows, pony races, even boxing matches.

The company would even build your cottage, complete with hardwood floors, stone fireplace, running water, and electricity. The appearance was rustic, but the modern comfort level was high.

In the 1960s, Bella Vista became less a weekend and summer home retreat. Today, it is owned and managed by Cooper Corporation, developers of Cherokee Village in the eastern Ozarks. Its emphasis is on permanent retirement homes.

This late 1920s postcard (above) shows a riding party in front of their Bella Vista summer retreat. Built on a narrow, steep lot, the typical summer home extended out from the hillside on a lattice-enclosed foundation.

CAMPS
FOR BOYS
FOR GIRLS

The idea that good character can be formed with exposure to the great outdoors is a cherished American belief. The wooded hills and clear streams of the Ozarks are an ideal setting for Arcadian activities of all kinds. Millions of Midwestern youths have attended the hundreds of summer camps in the region.

Archery, riflery, tennis, surfboat riding, swimming, and canoeing were favored activities. Instruction in dramatics, dancing, leather and wood working were available at some. Campers enjoyed special side trips to nearby wonders of nature and historical sites. A late 1930s Playgrounds Association yearbook (above) listed camps such as Gypsy Camp for Girls, near Siloam Springs, Arkansas, and the Joyzelle Camp for Girls at Monte Ne.

In the 1920s, Coca-Cola (right) commissioned an artist to capture the Arcadian atmosphere of the Boy Scout camp near Ironton, Missouri.

A scene near the Boy Scout Camp at Irondale in the Missouri Ozark Mountains, where each summer 2,000 Scouts get better acquainted with the great outdoors.

The best of good scouts must
come to a halt
—pause and refresh themselves

MERRILY they swing down the road early in the morning. Squirrels chattering. Birds singing. But Old Sol soon catches up. Hot and dusty grows the road. Tiring the miles. Squirrels and birds rest in the shade. Then the welcome signal, "Halt!" "I-yi-yi!" On the road side the little red Coca-Cola sign answers the watchword, "Be Prepared."

Stretched on the grass with such a drink—that's when a fellow knows what *the pause that refreshes* really means. ▸ ▸ So it is everywhere. You find Coca-Cola ready ice-cold wherever thirst calls and whenever a pause will mean the most. That tingling, delicious taste and its cool after-sense of refreshment packs a big rest into a little minute and gets you off to a fresh start.

THE BEST SERVED DRINK IN THE WORLD
A pure drink of natural flavors served ice-cold in its own glass and in its own bottle: The crystal thin Coca-Cola glass that represents the best in soda fountain service. The distinctive Coca-Cola bottle you can always identify; it is sterilized filled and sealed air-tight without the touch of human hands, insuring purity and wholesomeness. The Coca-Cola Company, Atlanta, Ga.

LISTEN IN—Grantland Rice—Famous Sports Champions—Coca-Cola Orchestra—Wed. 10:30 to 11 p. m. Eastern Daylight Saving Time—Coast to Coast NBC Network

NINE MILLION A DAY

Guests wrote a brief account of their stay. The press published a lavishly illustrated booklet of these 1920s testimonials to vigorous outdoor living and communing with nature as practiced at the retreat. Dedicated "To our Employees, our Friends … and to the ideal of human betterment," President Von Hoffmann and Vice President Williams put forth a virtual declaration of Arcadian principals:

May the book refresh memories of carefree days spent in the verdant luxury of this Ozark Valley, where the song birds frolic amid the rustling leaves in joy at the mere fact of living; where their music blends with the cadence of rippling, crystal streams and the soft soughing of the winds through the treetops and where gentle evening zephyrs bring quietude and grateful repose.

The onward trend of civilization has sent the Red Man from

As well as commercial resorts, individuals and occasionally companies built retreats in the Ozarks. Mihaska was the essence of Ozark Arcadianism. Within 2,600 mostly forested acres near Bourbon, Missouri, a successful St. Louis printing company, Von Hoffmann Press, maintained a resort for its employees and select guests. They stayed in log and stone cabins and could hike, ride horses, and boat on the nearby Meramec River. Rainbow trout were raised in a hatchery. A pond was stocked with bass. The zoo was popular with visitors' children. A model farm supplied milk, bacon and eggs. Harmony between man and nature, employer and employee, was the ideal.

The guest list included the governor and secretary of state of Missouri, the mayor of St. Louis, important printing clients, editors of magazines and newspapers, bank presidents, many union officers, judges, the St. Louis police commissioner, and Game and Fish Department officials. Even the president of a St. Louis labor union could, after a stay at Mihaska, wax eloquent about leaping trout, wild flowers, and chirping birds.

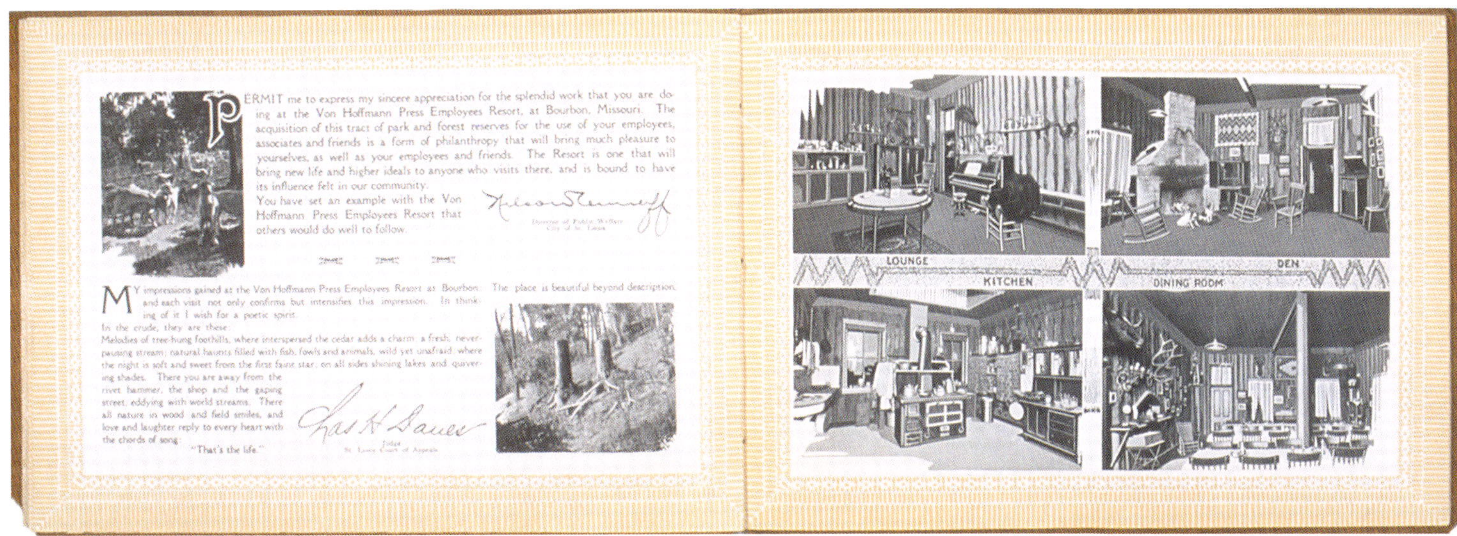

the scene, but Dame Nature continues to smile upon and lavish her beauty on Mi-has-ka. May the enchanting beauty of the Von Hoffman Press Employees' Resort awaken appreciation for the better things of life and bring inspiration for higher ideals and deeper gratitude for the glorious works of the Maker. Here employer and employee are alike and equal in enjoyment of the lavished bounty of nature and here they play together in practical demonstration of the real brotherhood of man and the democracy of industry.

Superintendent of the U.S. Bureau of Fisheries, Fred J. Foster, extolled the retreat's appeal.

Nature must have designed this Eden as a place of rest and recreation for her favorite companions. Its limpid springs, singing brooks, beautiful meadows and verdure clad-hills would awaken the heart of a poet, the eye of an artist and the mind of a philosopher in the most prosaic soul.

To A. J. Child, president of A. J. Child Mercantile Company,

It all seems like a dream and yet so real. Those who have enjoyed the splendid outing and treat, wait and hope to be invited again to Mihaska—land of dreams, home of rainbow trout and land of the free.

Missouri Secretary of State, Charles U. Bedcer, saw the Arcadian pleasures of Mihaska as a solution to labor/management conflict.

If more of our wealthy business men would follow in the footsteps of the Von Hoffman Press in taking care of their employees I am sure there would be less discontentment among employees in the great plants of this country.

BIG SPRINGS COUNTRY

Big Springs Country has a lot to see, but the best scenery must be observed from a canoe seat. The region's famous spring-fed rivers have cut deep valleys that made road building difficult. Tourist developments – unlike Eureka Springs, Branson, and Lake of the Ozarks – are minimal. That's fine with generations of floaters, fishermen, hunters, and nature lovers who cherish the region's primitive, still relatively inaccessible wild character.

Rushing and racing down thru this wonderland of Nature, fed by the largest springs in the United States, flows the beautiful Current River… Peering into its transparent depths, the fisherman sees, many feet below him, the cleanly washed gravel of its bottom with here and there a darting bass to be outwitted by the cunning art of the fly fisherman. Our wooded hills and Current River abound in game and fish that have survived the onrush of civilization.

The region has many karst features, like caves, but most are too remote for touristic development. Meramec Caverns (souvenir pillow cover, above) is close to I-44 (formerly U.S. 66) and has been a popular attraction for decades.

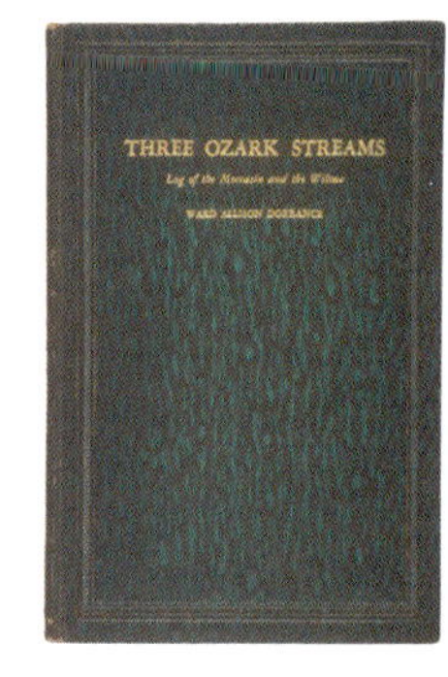

Fed by great springs, the streams of the region have a magical clarity. All visitors marvel, but in a scarce, self-published 1937 book, *Three Ozark Streams*, Ward Allison Dorrance put in words the mystical qualities of the cold, clear flowing water.

The water of the Black, as a matter of fact, is as transparent as water in a tumbler, taking on numerous hues according to its depth and according to the hour of the sun. In deep places it is blue. These enviable poets, the natives, have the phrase "to strike blue water" – to come upon a fishing pool. In the shallows it is leaf green, mottled with the tan and olive of sand and rocks. Where shallow merges into deep, it is the color of the ocean. At sunset it runs apple-green, lemon, and rose, turning nacre in the reflections of the willows, where the afterglow no longer strikes. This chameleon power (together with its speed and clarity) makes of the river a living thing, a third friend present. The day when I see it speeding out of its mist at dawn can not be like another day.

As the map (right) shows, the 14-county Big Springs region nearly touches St. Louis. Many of that city's companies were involved in early Ozark timbering and mining enterprises. Other St. Louisans have been dedicated to conservation efforts. The Missouri Ozarks Chamber of Commerce was primarily a St. Louis-based group that promoted an enlightened form of resource development and tourism based on scenic beauty, historic interest, and primitive recreation. Launched in the hard times of the 1930s, the group failed to stimulate much tourism, but did influence government policies.

Big Springs Country contains some of Missouri's earliest and finest state parks and large tracts of national and state forests. In 1964, the nation's first National Scenic River was dedicated, preserving the Current and Jacks Fork rivers in a wild state. This was due in part to the efforts of such early, wise-land-use advocates. These groups recognized 80 years ago the natural beauty of this part of the Ozarks and the need to preserve its scenic features and primitive character.

The Civilian Conservation Corps (CCC) was a New Deal federal works project that planted pines in national forests and constructed attractive rustic structures (opposite page) in state parks.

All-weather roads penetrated the semi-wilderness regions of the Ozarks in the 1930s. In a Missouri State Game and Fish Department pamphlet, tourists are invited to see Missouri's newly accessible state parks, many in the Big Springs region. For only $1 to $1.50 a day, one could stay in a rustic cabin built by the Civilian Conservation Corps from plans supplied by the National Parks Service. Modern highways and better accommodations are mentioned, but readers are reassured that these have not altered the primitive character of the region.

With all the development of physical properties upon the park areas, not one tree or flower was damaged, could it be saved. A cardinal rule in the developing of these playgrounds has been one of conservation. The parks have retained their natural backwoods character while furnishing the most modern conveniences.

The last page of this booklet is an invitation to visit written in pure Arcadian prose.

Now, you have read what the parks and forests offer to you. Why not picture YOURSELF on vacation in one of these playgrounds?

Imagine the glory of the Ozarks at eventide where down on the stream below your retreat the fading sunlight is tossed from the overhanging sycamores. With the light gone from

The great springs, isolated and inaccessible, were scarcely utilized during the spa era when spring water was widely held to have miraculous medical benefits. Their astonishing beauty did not go unnoticed. Indians held them sacred. The drama of millions of gallons of ice cold, crystal clear water pouring out of a deep azure basin is poorly depicted in old postcards. This tinted photograph of Big Spring (left) from the *Parks and Playgrounds* booklet is esthetically more successful. Even better is seeing such a natural spectacle. Many of the great springs have been preserved in a natural state as Missouri state parks or as part of the federal Ozark National Scenic Riverways.

*the upper end of the valley the stream is left to fade into
a purple veil.*

*The roof of an old grist mill, all that can be seen through
the ancient trees from the knob, is splashed with saffron.
While you watch, the yellow glow slips from the roof of the
mill, slithers off the bridge on the stream below and up the
cabins in the area. The retreating sunlight becomes a great
painter sweeping the valley with one deft stroke that trails
in its wake pigments of orange and brown and blue-green
to blend into shadowy purples.*

A pleasant picture, isn't it?

The latchstring is out—and you're invited.

**Early settlers utilized the energy of the rushing spring
water to power mills which primarily ground corn.
Alley Springs Mill (right) on the Jacks Fork River has
been preserved with its milling machinery intact.**

**This excellent 1949 booklet by the Missouri State
Division of Resources and Development (below right)
illustrated the survival of early American music and
basket weaving in Big Springs Country.**

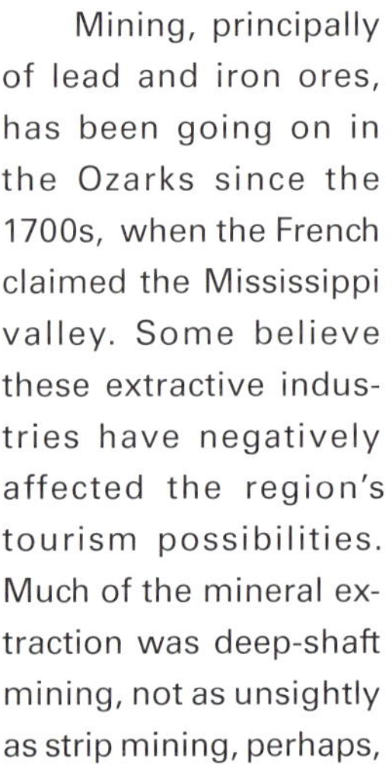

Mining, principally of lead and iron ores, has been going on in the Ozarks since the 1700s, when the French claimed the Mississippi valley. Some believe these extractive industries have negatively affected the region's tourism possibilities. Much of the mineral extraction was deep-shaft mining, not as unsightly as strip mining, perhaps, but problematic nevertheless. While evidence can still be found of 200-year-old lead working, the appearance today over much of the area is pastoral or forested.

Barytes, or tiff ore, is found near the surface in the northeastern section of the region. Tiff ore is a component of paint and ink, but most is utilized in oil drilling.

Nestling in their beds amidst the foothills of the Ozark Mountains these ore deposits lie restlessly in a region of piquant historical interest and of a natural scenic beauty. These lines are from an artistic and curiously candid booklet published in 1920 by the DeLore Baryta Company of St. Louis. Original paintings and drawings by famous St. Louis-born artist, O. E. Berninghaus, illustrated this booklet. It depicts the unsightly mining efforts by ragged but colorful and "happy, sturdy, primitive individuals," many of French colonial ancestry. Tiff mining was at best a messy operation. Modern mechanized extraction has further despoiled the landscape of Washington County.

The economic history of Big Springs Country may intrigue some visitors almost as much as its scenic beauty. Conservation groups do justifiably worry, however, about the environmental consequences of new mining.

Along the major streams – the St. Francis, Black, Current, Jacks Fork, and Meramec rivers – were small resorts of a rustic nature. Most were little more than a few rock or log cabins with cooking facilities and an ice box. Johnboats were tied up by the river for the use of guests. The office sold bait, soda, and the makings of a picnic. As these Depression-era snapshots show, such unpretentious, Mom-and-Pop enterprises have been the site of much affordable enjoyment.

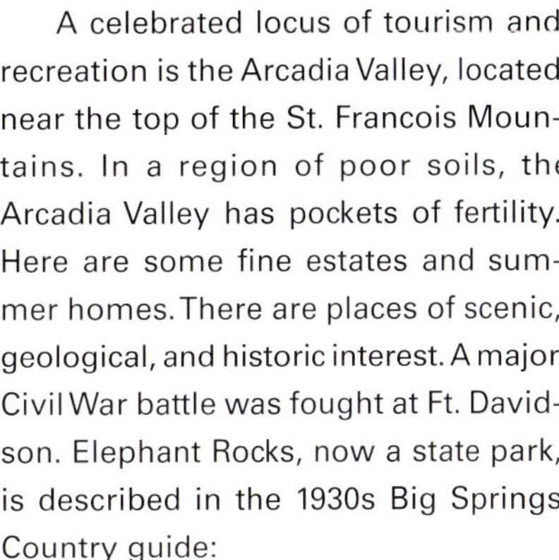

A celebrated locus of tourism and recreation is the Arcadia Valley, located near the top of the St. Francois Mountains. In a region of poor soils, the Arcadia Valley has pockets of fertility. Here are some fine estates and summer homes. There are places of scenic, geological, and historic interest. A major Civil War battle was fought at Ft. Davidson. Elephant Rocks, now a state park, is described in the 1930s Big Springs Country guide:

On a high point commanding an extensive view are huge granite boulders weighing many tons which have been cut into fantastic shapes by the elements during countless ages. One is known as "Elephant Rock." One of the narrow passages is known as "Fat Man's Misery." In grandeur it is said to rival the "Garden of the Gods" of Colorado.

LAKE OF THE OZARKS

Bagnell was a tiny village on the Osage River, on the northern edge of the Ozark uplift. In 1929, just months before the Wall Street crash, a huge dam was begun three miles upriver. Over 20,000 men would labor on this concrete engineering feat. It was completed in April 1931, and the silt-laden waters of the Osage, which rises in the Kansas prairie, began to fill Lake of the Ozarks.

Politicians wanted the large lake that backed up the Osage to be named either Lake Benton, after the famous nineteenth-century Missouri state senator, or Lake McClurg, after a former governor who hailed from the region. "Lake of the Ozarks" conceivably sounded less partisan to the builder, Union Electric Light and Power Co. Some 30 years later, Democrats finally got to name a water resource project on the upper Osage after one of their own: Truman Dam and Lake, just above the headwaters of Lake of the Ozarks. It was paid for by the federal government.

Souvenir tablecloth (right), 1950, illustrates Lake of the Ozarks' characteristic dragon-like shape.

Missouri's Great Lake Of The Ozarks
KANSAS CITY
HOLDEN
WARRENSBURG
SEDALIA
WINDSOR
LINCOLN
COLE CAMP
STOVER
EDMONSON
WARSAW
PROCTOR TOWERSITE
GRAVOIS MILLS
PURVIS
HASTAIN
EDWARDS
BARNUMTON
CLIMAX SPRINGS
FRISTOE
COLUMBIA
BOONEVILLE
MISSOURI R.
CALIFORNIA
JEFFERSON CITY
VERSAILLES
BARNETT
Y.M.C.A. CAMP
ELDON
LAKESIDE
TUSCUMBIA
BAGNELL DAM
OSAGE BEACH
KAISER
KAISER TOWER
BRUMLEY
CAMDENTON
LINN CREEK
ROACH
MONTREAL
STOUTLAND
HA HA TONKA
TUNNEL DAM
BENNETT SPRING STATE PARK
LEBANON
MEXICO
FULTON
WARRENTON
ST. CHARLES
TO ST. LOUIS
WASHINGTON
UNION
VIENNA
VICHY
ROLLA
IBERIA
ARLINGTON
SALEM
TO SPRINGFIELD
OZARK WOODLAND TRAILS
MISSOURI STATE CAPITOL JEFFERSON CITY, MO.
COPYRIGHTED 1950
SIMMONS & CARR ELDON, MO.

Bagnell Dam's purpose was hydro-electric generation for the lead mining industry and urban residential needs. The St. Louis company spent $30 million building the dam and acquiring the land it would flood. Work went on night and day. When finished, it was the largest artificial lake in the United States, 195 miles long with over 1,300 miles of shoreline.

Recreational use was contemplated by its builders, but that enterprise got off to a slow start. As the lake filled with water, the Great Depression deepened. Next, World War II cast a drab shadow on travel and leisure activities. Only with postwar prosperity did tourist development begin to steadily increase. One stimulus to development was the fact that houses and resorts could be built right on the water's edge. U.S. Army Corps of Engineers' lakes, like Table Rock and Bull Shoals, do not permit this.

Before Bagnell Dam, the region had little of the rustic tourism tradition of the White River Country. Lake of the Ozarks has a different history. A touristic culture quite distinct from that of the Branson/Shepherd of the Hills region resulted.

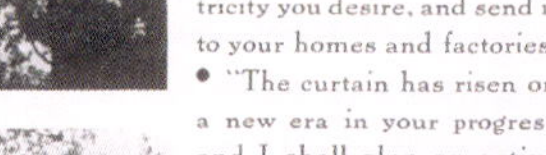

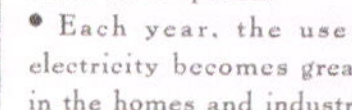

• Journey, for a moment, backward along the highroad of fancy to the early days of our country—to the lands of the Mississippi Valley.

• March with LaSalle and Lewis and Clark—and in your imagination, explore the Ozark Highlands—ancestral hunting ground of the Osage tribes.

• You see a beautiful land of wooded hills and valleys—of rivers and streams—watercourses that have been the avenues of exploration and the highways of settlement—passive factors in the growth of a nation.

• Passive? Yes—but man says "I want electricity—it is the servant that lessens my toil and promotes my comfort"—and the river answers, "I have carried your canoes to new lands and I have been a pathway to your villages and towns.

• "I shall generate the electricity you desire, and send it to your homes and factories.

• "The curtain has risen on a new era in your progress and I shall plan an active role." Thus might the Osage River have spoken.

• Each year, the use of electricity becomes greater in the homes and industries

The role of railroads as carriers of vacationing passengers had diminished by the 1930s. Passenger railroad service never reached the lake itself. Automobile recreationalists were, in general, more mobile and less nature-oriented than earlier tourists had been. From the beginning, Lake of the Ozarks was heralded as a powerboat paradise.

The little vignettes of genteel, country club-type activities from a 1930s booklet illustrate the high-style recreational development Union Electric envisioned for its new lake. Tennis anyone?

Lake of the Ozarks tourism has not often themed the past. No literature came to characterize the country around Lake of the Ozarks and its native folks the way Harold Bell Wright's *Shepherd of the Hills* imaged the folk culture of the White River hills. Bucolic fiction and local color writing or promotion about Lake of the Ozarks are rare.

Linn Creek, the county seat of Camden County, was within the new lake's pool. Its flooding engendered some nostalgic newspaper accounts, a poem or two, and a few postcards.

The saga of Ha-Ha-Tonka comes as close as anything to a Lake of the Ozarks legend. The Robert Snyder family of Kansas City built a stone castle on an incredible piece of real estate containing caves and a great spring which once fed a stream stocked with trout. The stream is now largely inundated by Lake of the Ozarks. The castle burned in 1940. The splendid, rain-polished ruins are now the centerpiece of a state park.

*"Clem! Can you picture all this land
Under the water? - where we stand
Right now? and all the entire town
- Even the Court House?"*
   – Waters Over Linn Creek Town
      Ralph Allan McCanse, 1951

The new lake's promotional literature was less mystical about nature than earlier railroad literature advertising Lake Taneycomo. There are only a few superlatives used to describe the "mystery" of this "outdoor wonderland" in the 1930s pamphlet (right). Mostly, it lists resorts, where to get beer and lunch, and presents glowing profiles of the small towns that hoped to cash in on the anticipated tourist boom.

The region's rustic heritage was largely confined to rock-faced buildings and a few log cabins. The new lake's roadside developments came a half century later than the beginnings of the White River's tourist industry. Arcadianism, by the 1930s, was more of a style than a belief.

Bagnell Dam itself was an object of curiosity, even as it was being built. Motorists flocked to witness concrete progress come to the slumbering northern Ozark hills. Union Electric built a

splendid boat dock by the dam and sold tickets for motor launch cruises. Afterwards, a fountain Coke and a sandwich could be had in the nearby, architect-designed Casino (without gambling) Restaurant, a company enterprise as well.

Plans of the utility company to monopolize the tourist trade came to a halt when the federal government ordered divestiture of all activities unrelated to their charter to provide electricity. Private development gradually filled in along Highway 54 between

the dam and Camdenton, the new county seat that replaced submerged Old Linn Creek.

In those lean, early years, fishing camps were started all over the lake. Floating boat docks evolved to accommodate changing lake levels. From the beginning, the lake was a powerboat paradise.

Boating is an ace pleasure. The Lake is credited with having more pleasure boats than any other inland body of water in the nation, except the great lakes. Every type of boat imaginable ply its water, a great fleet of private cruisers, houseboats, excursion and sight seeing craft of every description and thousands of fishing boats.

        – Lake of the Ozarks Association Guide, 1930s.

Early on, the complex pattern of Lake of the Ozark's shoreline was noted.

Like a Chinese Dragon, the Lake of the Ozarks twists and winds for one hundred and twenty-nine miles among the rolling foothills of the Ozark Highlands.

        – 1930s Union Electric pamphlet

Trophy bass came from the new lake, but not as humongous as this 1935 largemouth parade float (right). It was made by Lake of the Ozarks Post 193 of the American Legion.

US 54 Over Bagnell Dam, Lake of The Ozarks, Mo.
BAGNELL DAM
LAKE OF THE OZARKS
An Achievement of American Business Enterprise
Dedicated to the Service of the Public
UNION ELECTRIC COMPANY OF MISSOURI
EXCURSION BOAT RIDES
Niangua Bridge over The Lake of The Ozarks, Mo.
Horse Shoe Bend on The Lake of The Ozarks, Mo.
Souvenir Views of
LAKE OF THE OZARKS, MO.
Lake of the Ozarks
Resort Guide and Map
1937
Scenic View of The Lake of The Ozarks, Mo.
Aerial View of Bagnell Dam, Lake of The Ozarks, Mo.
"Lovers Leap" overlooking The Lake of The Ozarks
New Niangua Bridge over The Lake of The Ozarks, Mo.
Grand Glaize Bridge near Osage

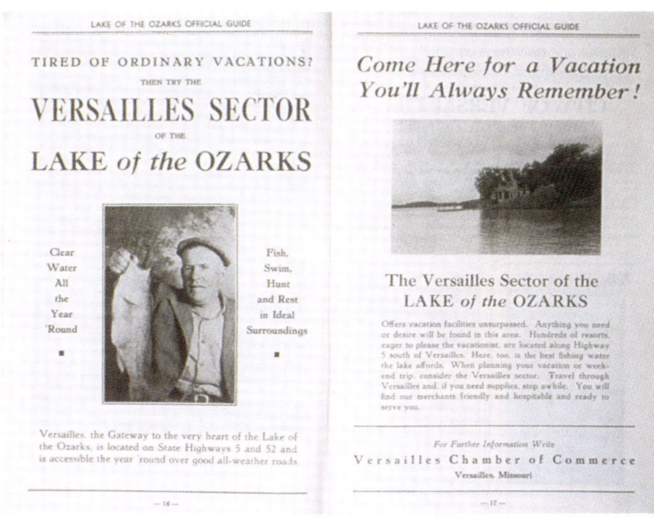

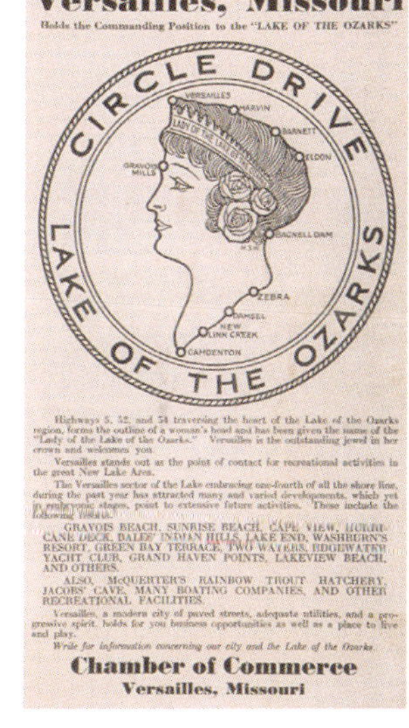

The area of greatest commercial development is south of where U.S. 54 crosses Bagnell Dam. Even before the post World War II boom, however, there were several hundred mostly family-run, small resorts on the lake. Fishing camps and summer resorts sprang up through the 1930s on the upper, and generally clearer, arms of the lake. All the small towns close to the new reservoir claimed to be the "Gateway to the Lake of the Ozarks." Villages like Versailles were not transformed into metropolises, but local businesses often felt a stimulating effect. Even before the lake filled, the Morgan County newspaper published a little promotional booklet (above): *Versailles Missouri: The Open Door to the Center of the $30,000,000 Lake of the Ozarks Project.*

Versailles will be surrounded by the beauty spots of the Ozarks, with locations for summer cottages, with ideal camping and fishing locations where man may profit by one of the greatest industrial developments of the age without sacrificing nature, the picturesque vistas of the winding valleys and rugged hills.

The iconic dam and too-blue waters are features of 1930s Lake of the Ozarks souvenirs. Technicolor sunsets and 3-D letters enhance picture postcards and maps. We almost hear travelogue music swell as we read the ad copy. – *It is truly the sportsman's paradise, the tired man's retreat and the end of the artist's dream.*

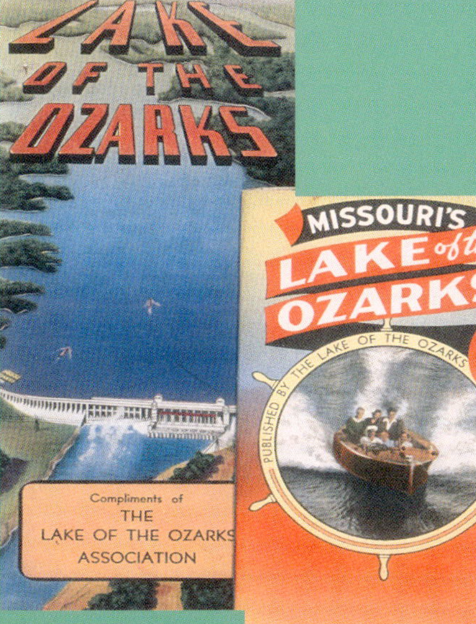
LAKE OF THE OZARKS
MISSOURI'S
LAKE of the OZARKS
PUBLISHED BY THE LAKE OF THE OZARKS ASSOCIATION
Compliments of
THE LAKE OF THE OZARKS ASSOCIATION
Compliments of
THE LAKE OF THE OZARKS ASSOCIATION

"PLAYGROUND OF THE MIDDLE-WEST"
LAKE OF THE OZARKS IN MISSOURI
PLACE STAMP HERE
Souvenir of the
LAKE of the OZARKS IN MISSOURI
ONE OF THE WORLD'S LARGEST ARTIFICIAL LAKES
POSTAGE 1½¢ WITHOUT MESSAGE
Greetings From
MISSOURI'S GREAT Lake of the Ozarks COUNTRY
LAKE OF THE OZARKS

The "Larry-Don" Excursion Boat, Lake of the Ozarks, Missouri

Excursion Boat "Gov. McClurg," Lake of the Ozarks, Missouri

Greetings from
LAKE OF THE OZARKS
MISSOURI

HIGH DAMS AND MODERN TIMES

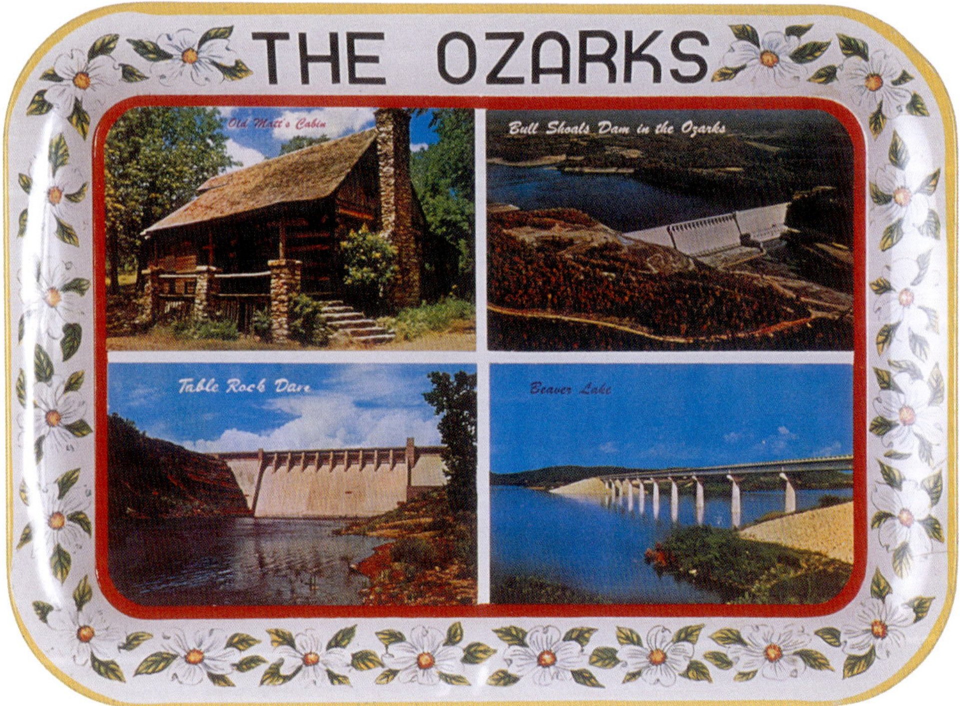

Progress, in the shape of great government dams and modernized highways, came to the Ozarks in the decades after World War II. Even the back country felt the prop wash of prosperity. A surge of shiny new Detroit cars, packed with little baby boomers, headed out of the suburbs each summer for the obligatory summer vacation in the "Playground of the Middle West".

"Lunkers for everyone," proclaimed the happy tourist in the Ozark Vacationland montage on the opposite page. Travel became democratized. In an era of big government, big business, and mass media, recreation became more standardized. Consumerism was the order of the day.

Image, while not immune to changing circumstance, is often persistent. Public perceptions of the Ozarks remained rooted in earlier versions of its real, or fictitious, Arcadian past. Primitivist imagery and poetic language hung on in tourist promotions.

Souvenirs and promotional materials of the era mixed icons of the rustic past with images of a new, altered landscape. If paradoxical, such juxtaposition of the traditional and industrial have not slowed the growth of Ozark tourism.

THE OZARK'S FAMILY VACATIONLAND
World Famous White River
Float Trip
Lake Taneycomo
Free Ferry, U. S. 62, Norfork Lake
Beautiful Blanchard Springs
Lunkers for Everyone
Golf
Riding the Waves

After announcing the transformation of the White River into a man-made paradise by government dams, a 1950s map (left) lapses into some retro-Arcadian prose.

With every knowledge of existing world chaos, this section of Ozarkland continues to provide a refuge from the stress and strain of today's urban life, for in this sanctuary of rounded hills one may regain an undistracted mind. Here each newborn day cries out in exaltation at the joy of life ahead. Each setting sun trails rosy fingers caressingly across the velvet hills, to disappear at last and leave a quivering earth to calm and to lie in a languor, awaiting the gentle kiss of the great white Ozark moon.

Such languid prose was better suited to describing a canoe gliding down a tree-lined river. The tourism business has not yet found a literary style suited to capturing the ambience of motorboats on a reservoir.

Not only was the landscape of the Ozarks modified by dams, roads, and continuing mining and logging, but the American attitude toward nature was also changing. Many of the new visitors

In the new manmade lakes, the heftier largemouth black bass replaced the river-loving smallmouth bass. Fishing was, at first, phenomenal. In time, catch-and-release tournaments were organized with prizes like pro bass boats, a craft that was developed in Ozark Corps of Engineers' impoundments.

were disinterested in communing with nature. Vacations were for pure diversion and pleasure. Comfort tourism supplanted rustic outings.

Arcadianism did not vanish, however. Hunters and fishermen remained true to the belief that there are transcendental aspects to outdoor sports. Conservation became the philosophy of these sportsmen, and the government agencies and organizations that regulated and represented them.

Other nature lovers became highly critical of development and technology, in general. Radicalized and politicized Arcadians created the ecology movement, often at odds with conservationists, as well as with the industrial state.

Many of the earlier Ozark Arcadians coexisted with tourists and sportsmen, even promoting those utilizations. Vance Randolph, the folklorist, hunted and fished with the hillfolk, and wrote of these adventures in books and sporting magazines.

River guide George Foster wrote an elegiac poem (left) about the loss of the lower James River to Table Rock Dam and Lake.

FAREWELL BEAUTIFUL JAMES RIVER

I am just an old broke down river rat,
Have a story I want to tell,
How they're fixin' to ruin our beautiful stream
I tell you folks, it's h--l!
Now, you can take old Mother Nature,
She has done her work with care,
Then take Man's beautiful pictures,
You see, it's nothing to compare.
I know this old river like a book,
Almost to every rock and tree,
But I have been floating it for forty odd years, you see.
Many and many a night I have camped on her nice clean gravel bars,
Sleeping out in the wide open spaces beneath the bright shining stars,
So come all you good fishers, and float while you may,
I hope to see you at Camp Rock Haven, at the Fisherman's Hat Cafe!
Written for Camp Rock Haven—By River Rat George Foster
(Rock Haven Guide)

Mail Address Route No. 3
Galena, Missouri

Flood control, not recreation, was the primary rationale for the 15 Army Corps of Engineers reservoirs built from the 1930s to the 1960s in the Ozarks. Taneycomo (1912) and Lake of the Ozarks (1931) were private hydropower projects. During the Depression, the Roosevelt administration expanded the federal government into many formerly capitalistic spheres. Dam-building was attractive to advocates of a centrally planned economy and an engineered society. Politicians loved the high visibility of these multi-million-dollar public works projects.

Jim Owens and others in the float business opposed them, of course, as did farmers whose lands would be inundated. On the other hand, local businessmen generally welcomed the economic stimulus and new tourist draw.

They have been busy beavers. Virtually every stream in the Ozarks (and the country, for that matter) has a Corps-authorized dam site. Growing environmental objections, as well as spiraling costs and unprovable benefits, have slowed the dam-building juggernaut. Truman Dam (originally Kaysinger Bluff Dam) was challenged by lawsuits, but was completed. It may be the last massive water resource project to be built in the region.

In the 1960s, a coalition of local landowners and environmentalists did stop the construction of a Corps dam on the Meramec River. Two of the Ozarks most celebrated free-flowing streams, the Current and Buffalo rivers, were designated National Scenic Riverways to prevent their being dammed.

Fed by clear Ozark rivers, the waters of these lakes are of high quality and clarity. Attractive as the lakes may be to many, Corps pamphlets set no new standards in promotional literature.

Stockton Lake is located in an area which offers a great deal to the outdoors enthusiast…In this typical Ozark setting, man has joined with nature to provide a 24,900 acre lake with a shoreline of about 300 miles…It is hoped that your visit will be pleasant and safe and that you will return often in the future.

It may be unfair to expect soaring metaphors from engineers led by army officers. Still, the old time sporting writers might wonder if this was the same Ozarks they had described so well, and with such passion.

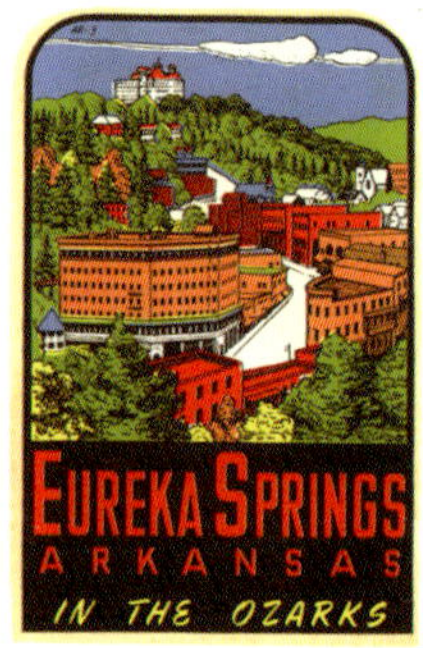

In the atomic '50s, the psychedelic '60s, and the synthetic '70s, the hues of Ozark touristic imagery fairly glowed. Intensified color schemes did not necessarily mean the Ozark recreational product had changed. Eureka Springs's grand old limestone buildings were still a soft, weathered gray, not orange, as in the decal. The trout stream at Montauk was not lined by chrome yellow trees.

Already a caricature, Ozark natives were further stylized by modern graphics. Generic hillbillies decorated matchbooks, postcards, and decals. The Great Society's war on poverty took no prisoners. Once seen as independent, hillfolk were decaled as poverty-stricken rural vagrants.

A television set floats ominously above Johnson Shut-ins. This 1956 Missouri Division of Resources and Development pamphlet is an as-seen-on-TV classic. Students of mid-twentieth-century banality will find inside a treasury of posed kodachromes and clichéd captions. "Variety is the keyword in your Missouri vacation. Rippling waterfalls are part of the diversity."

Western Missouri Land-O-Lakes Association

Small towns on the northwestern Ozark border near the new Corps lakes published a 'mod' orange colored booklet (left) hoping to attract a somewhat contradictory mix of tourists, retirees, and industry.

This fabulously beautiful country of clear streams, deep valleys, and picturesque heavily timbered hills covers an area of over 30,000 square miles. The Ozarks is also the home of such famous Caverns as Meramec, Onondaga, Bridal, and Marvel. This region is world renowned for fine fishing and hunting – truly a sportsmans paradise. You will find here the famous "Shepherd of the Hills" Country made immortal by the pen of Harold Bell Wright. You will remember forever the scenic splendor of the beautiful country – once having been here.

Popular culture's touristic destination is never-never land. Earlier Arcadian travel promotion floated tourists down moonlit rivers of flowing ad copy, but it also produced real photo postcards of real locations. Though hardly realistic, *The Shepherd of the Hills* has social and geographic specificities, compared to the escapism of modern mass entertainment. Harold Bell Wright's 1907 novel may have journeyed a bit down the path to kitsch, but his book depicts a geo-cultural province with recognizable characters and places.

This charming, 1950s Lake of the Ozarks scarf (above) includes Lake Taneycomo and Turner's Mill, not attractions within that region. Hopefully, the awesome ability of mass culture to create stunning graphics compensates for its neglect of geography and other old-fashioned, hard-core literacies.

Not all post-war Ozark touristic graphics were so indifferent to actual appearance. The subtler souvenir plate (right) by Vernon Kilns of California has a montage of scenes and attractions realistically rendered. On the back is more traditional description of the "Land of the Ozarks."

Alley Spring Grist Mill

Alley Spring and the adjacent mill one of the most beautiful sites to behold while visiting Eminence, Missouri. Our vintage town, founded 1868, sits along side the crystal clear Jacks Fork River and has much to offer the visitor. Just 12 miles north of Highway 60 and 75 miles south of Highway 44, the scenic drive to Eminence along Highway 19 is even more splendid when spring dogwoods are in bloom or fall leaves are in full color.

The reputation of the Ozarks, at the start of the 21st century, is not unlike its promotions of long ago. What attracted our ancestors then, moves us now. In spite of efforts to modernize the region, much of it is still relatively natural or pastoral. Even those travelers who want an abundance of creature comforts report they are appreciative of the natural beauty of the hill country.

Post World War II advertising, facing greater competition for the visitor's attention, is characteristically bolder, brighter, and less likely to extol the region in Arcadian hyperbole. The brilliantly colored rack cards sing out for attention, but they don't tell the whole story. The first half-century of Ozark promotion, chronicled in *See The Ozarks*, better illustrates the region's perennial allure. Modern times, in the form of fast food chains and strip shopping centers, are here, as everywhere. But such development doesn't, for the most part, obscure the back country character of the place. Ozark recreation still has an outdoorsy, rural, and small-town flavor; an Ozark vacation still provides a reprieve from urban complexities.

While the "Shepherd of the Hills Country" label is rarely used to refer to the White River hills anymore, Branson and Ozark Mountain Country cling steadfastly to their family focus in both ad copy and entertainment offerings. Eureka Springs, grande dame of the region, has been restored to her Victorian charms.

Millions of acres of forest, in a natural or preserved state, offer solitude or wild adventure in the Boston Mountains and Big Springs Country. Now, bed-and-breakfast accommodations, as well as streamside camping, are available for floaters. Writers for national sporting magazines still extol, as they did in 1890, Ozark hunting and fishing possibilities.

Lake of the Ozarks, with its lack of shoreline restrictions, continues to build up with homes and condos. Each year there are more dining and shopping opportunities along the shore, and more and bigger boats on the water.

Subterranean mysteries of Ozark show caves continue to fascinate. Trains, no longer the primary conveyance for tourists to get to the region, now provide short, scenic excursions through the Ozark countryside.

Opportunities still abound for individuals wishing to relocate. The relatively flat Ozark plateau, especially the areas along old Route 66, and the prosperous northwest corner of Arkansas, are booming economically. Immediately adjacent to the unimproved, scenic lands, this area offers gainful employment close to recreation – an attractive combination. The Ozark Mountain region is ranked fifth on eBay's list of top land markets, based on the volume of unimproved land sold.

A majority of the businesses that cater to tourists and recreationalists are locally owned. Two of the most successful, Silver Dollar City and Bass Pro, have built on the foundation of past Ozark tourism.

Bass Pro has 16 Outdoor World mega-stores across the U.S., stocked with every conceivable product a fisherman, hunter, camper, or suburbanite could use. The Adirondack-rustic architecture of its flagship store in Springfield, Missouri is reminiscent of Ozark resorts of a century ago. Enlarged photos of early White River float trips decorate the showrooms. Founder John Morris's Ozarkian sensibilities are evident in other company ventures – Dogwood Canyon, "10,000 acres of Ozark Paradise," and Big Cedar Lodge, a restored and enlarged version of Devil's Pool Ranch near Branson. The American National Fish and Wildlife museum is located on property donated by Morris next to the Springfield store. McCanse and other pioneer Ozark conservationists would see continuity here.

Silver Dollar City, in Branson, is a living encyclopedia of the Arcadian era's take on pioneer times. It is an idealized 19th century Ozark village built at the entrance of Marvel Cave, a show cave opened to the public in 1894. The crafts, music, food, and folk ways of the Ozark frontier are re-created and reenacted here for millions of visitors every year. Contemporary amusements like roller coasters are styled to fit into the sylvan environment.

Silver Dollar City and Bass Pro have applied lessons learned from decades of Ozark tourism to their enterprises beyond the region. Silver Dollar City manages Dollywood in the Great Smoky Mountains and Stone Mountain in Atlanta, Georgia.

The region itself, and what people believe it can provide, remain much the same. It's low-key, low-cost, relaxed, friendly, and intimate. Never about any kind of excess, the Ozarkian experience offers natural beauty and an escape from modern tensions. *See The Ozarks,* yourself!

The Beautiful and Enduring Ozarks has a distinctly non-touristic perspective. Payton's photographs focus on wild rivers, back roads, villages, country churches, and farmers with sun-etched faces. Quotes from early explorers and geographers support his concept that the Ozarks has always been, and will likely remain, a cultural and ecological refuge from the changes that sweep over it.

A reader praised the book as "a crystallization, a naming of all that uniqueness as I find in the Ozarks...a modern classic."

Payton has an especially soft spot for local color, such as the hill-country characters made famous in the paintings of native Ozarker Thomas Hart Benton and whose descendants are still very much a part of the landscape. This quirky book is every bit as iconoclastic as the people and places Payton writes about and photographs.

– June Sawyers, The Resourceful Traveler, *Chicago Tribune*

The book is beautifully written, illustrated and put together. It does an excellent job of providing an understanding of the Ozarks. It gives one a feeling for the true Ozarks.

– Dr. Oscar (Oz) Hawksley, author of *Missouri Ozark Waterways*

It's the next best thing to being there. The way most of America was, it still is – in the Beautiful and Enduring Ozarks.

– Paul Harvey, on-air review

The text is both laugh-out-loud funny and quietly tender. It's the best way to show others ("fer'ners," that is) what they're missing in the Ozarks.

– Kate Klise, journalist and author

The Beautiful and Enduring Ozarks by Leland Payton. $19.95
139 photographs, 87 in full color
ISBN 0-9673925-0-0

If unavailable at your local bookstore, *See The Ozarks* and *The Beautiful and Enduring Ozarks* may be ordered from:

LENS & PEN PRESS
P.O. Box 14557
Springfield MO 65814

Add $4.00 S&H for 1 book, and $2.00 S&H for each additional book.

You may order online at
www.beautifulozarks.com

Leland Payton's evocative photographs of the natural Ozarks are available as limited edition prints. These archivally permanent images are printed on fine paper.

Select images from *See The Ozarks* are also available.

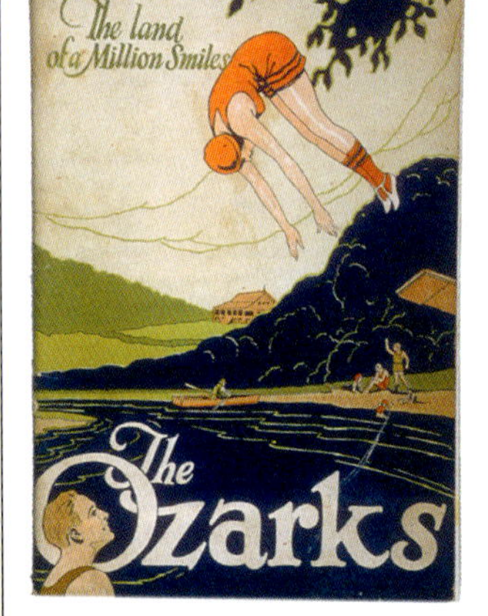

Prints may be viewed and purchased online at www.beautifulozarks.com